Transitional Objects in Early Childhood

In this innovative book, Amanda Norman looks at D. W. Winnicott's theory of Transitional Objects in early years practice, the 'good-enough' parent, and the relationship between the young child and primary carer in relation to the value of Transitional Objects.

Norman looks at how an understanding of psychological theories can be useful when caring for young children in both educational and research contexts, aiding those interested in understanding therapeutic relationships, and applying the principles to promote the use of Transitional Objects in their work. Throughout the book, Norman uses case studies from parents, children, and practitioner's perspectives in supporting physical and emotional development. Through these, she shows how observing Transitional Objects is particularly relevant to living in the West, where a low touch, high technology culture prevails, compounded by the recent pandemic. This volume contributes to a timely connection between the understanding and application of therapeutic approaches within early educational contexts. Including engaging exercises at the end of each chapter, this book is a perfect companion for those approaching the concept of Transitional Objects for the first time.

Transitional Objects in Early Childhood is vital reading for those with an interest in the psychology of the infant/young child and their relationship and realities with the external world. It will be of particular interest to those specialising in infant and child care who wish to develop their knowledge of emotional development through play, as well as those working in a variety of social, education, and health contexts.

Amanda Norman is a Senior Lecturer at the University of Winchester, UK. She is the author of two books and has published works about infant care pedagogies and emotional well-being in academic peer reviewed and professional practice articles. As a practising therapeutic play specialist and early years consultant she continues to support and liaise with early professionals working in the sector, in addition to her academic role.

Transitional Objects in Early Childhood

The Value of Transitional Objects in the Early Years

Amanda Norman

Routledge
Taylor & Francis Group

LONDON AND NEW YORK

Designed cover image: Amanda Norman.

First published 2024
by Routledge
4 Park Square, Milton Park, Abingdon, Oxon OX14 4RN

and by Routledge
605 Third Avenue, New York, NY 10158

Routledge is an imprint of the Taylor & Francis Group, an informa business

British Library Cataloguing-in-Publication Data
A catalogue record for this book is available from the British Library

ISBN: 978-1-032-28400-2 (hbk)
ISBN: 978-1-032-28047-9 (pbk)
ISBN: 978-1-003-29666-9 (ebk)

DOI: 10.4324/9781003296669

Typeset in Times New Roman
by Taylor & Francis Books

Contents

Figures

Introduction

Rationale

This introduction outlines the purpose of writing the book and its contribution to those professionally working with children within and beyond early care and educational (ECE) contexts. As a therapeutic play specialist and educator, Transitional Objects (TO) are explored with a focus on young children's health as their well-being continues to influence their sense of space, place, and relationships as we have emerged from the pandemic (2020). The content of this book therefore contributes to a timely connection between the understanding and application of therapeutic approaches within early childhood. Winnicott's (1951) 'good enough' mother (parent) and the relationship between the young child and primary carer is discussed in relation to the value of TO and how an understanding of psychological theories can be useful when caring for young children in educational and research contexts. The readership is for those with an interest in the psychology of the young child and their relationship and realities with the external world. It is also relevant for those specialising in infant and early care, seeking to increase their knowledge about emotional development. It includes topics for those interested in understanding therapeutic relationships, applying the principles to promoting the appreciation, understanding, and inclusion of TO in their work. It therefore aims to be a useful book resource, with informed practices included and case study examples provided, regarding the complexities and appreciation of TO. These are included from parents, children, and practitioner's perspectives in supporting physical and emotional development, particularly relevant to living in the West, where a low touch, high technological culture prevails, compounded by having lived experiences of a pandemic.

This book will focus primarily on Transitional Objects (TO) in early childhood, contextualised in ECE settings, which I will refer to as formal day care settings to ensure an international consideration to centres, nursery settings, family centres, and services in caring for and supporting young children. Themes and discussions will therefore include young children's transitional spaces and consistent primary carers, either from their home or the formal

DOI: 10.4324/9781003296669-1

day care setting they attend. A wider knowledge about the benefits of working in a multidisciplinary way aims to enhance an emotional understanding about young children. This book serves to bridge the clinical work around Winnicott's theory and concepts, extending the principles within formal day care. Theory of attachment and Object Relations will also be explored and examined in relation to understanding the value of TO.

By initially studying TO from a historical perspective, the ideas about sentimental objects and objects that have symbolic meaning to the parent and child are introduced. A discussion about the theory and then practice and thinking about TO today is then further explored and discussed. The latter chapters focus is on how objects, including TO can be researched in a creative way and how they remain part of an individual's sense of self and their connection to their past as well as their present external world around them.

The book is aimed at educators interested in childhood and psychology although relevant and valuable for practitioners working in a variety of formal day care settings and those with a specialist interest in Winnicott's work. It would also be of benefit to therapeutic play specialists or those curious about embarking on play therapy training. The main topics and subjects discussed will include the psychological and cultural perception of TO in understanding contemporary practice. There will be a focus on policy, and key figures that have influenced the use of TO and emotional development. In referring to other studies, theories, and practices, the chapters also aim to provide a contextualised introduction to those with more experience in psychotherapy or embarking on specialist training. Whilst there are many more books and studies with further, and arguably deeper analytical discourses and reflective thinking about Winnicott, this book's prime purpose is to introduce some thinking about TO and bridge those with limited knowledge. It therefore aims to provide a fruitful beginning to what I consider a fascinating ongoing journey into the world of Winnicott, his understanding about childhood, and how his work remains internationally relevant today.

Connections to Other Professions and Disciplines

The chapters include a link to past and current theories and approaches towards personal, social, and emotional learning and development, with reference to how the pandemic has created opportunities for reflection and considered ways of understanding and working with other professions including psychologists, counsellors, the nursing profession, and wider notions around material culture and worlding theory. The notion of 'worlding' arising from non-representational theory provides a useful lens through which the process of human-non-human enmeshment can be considered. Kathleen Stewart (2010) provides a definition of worlding referring to the 'affective nature' of the world in which 'non-human agency' comprising 'forms, rhythms and refrains', each a point of 'expressivity' for an individual, develops a sense of 'legibility'. Through this process, a particular 'world' emerges for the individual through their engagement with several interrelated phenomena. This is an area I resonate with and, as a Froebel inspired educator, the unity of life and connections to humans and non-humans is central to thinking about unity in all things, within nature (the external) and in spirit (the internal), with the two uniting together. Anderson and Harrison (2010) expand on worlding further by considering the term 'world' not to be an existing, living thing but rather the context or background against which things show up and take on significance. They consider it flowing but at the same time 'a stable ensemble of practices, involvements, relations, capacities, tendencies and affordances' (p. 8). Although it is argued that TO are more about the transitional space of the child's inner psyche, firmly grounded in the psychology of the child, there is a new materialist, post-humanist perspective, regarding the relationships between humans and non-humans. It provides an opportunity to delve deeper into the entangled human–world relations and the relationships between humans and non-humans. It also further considers what the immediately perceived experiences of the world might consist of, and how immediate encounters between humans and non-humans connect and intersect with the wider world. Worlding processes are considered beyond a set of physical or situational conditions. Rather, as Haraway (2008) affirms, it is about engaging in the continual processes of becoming with a world whereby the intertwinement of natures, cultures, subjects, and want is interesting for me in thinking about TO (p. 13).

The articulation of worlding processes is complex and Haraway (2008) alludes to the importance of articulation through selecting and applying the most relevant or appropriate terminology that might convey something of the human-non-human worlding. This includes what is considered and perceived as human and non-human matter, what counts and what matters and, through doing so enables the fostering of new ontological dispositions towards the world, forever evolving, unfinished and always on the move. Haraway (2016), as a post-humanist, also considers an ethical position that extends a moral concern to things that are different from us and specifically with other species and objects with which we cohabit the world. For me, in thinking about ethical positions in childhood it also helps us see ourselves as being interconnected rather than separate from non-human beings, and how we value the non-human aspects in our and young children's everyday life. Ultimately the idea around worlding is that it is personal and subjective according to the person who experiences the world around them. My own worlding would be unique to another. Worlding therefore is an active, ontological process and not simply a result of existence in or passive encounter with environments, circumstances, events or places. Worlding is informed by individual's focus of attention to a specific experience, place or encounter and the active engagement with the materiality and context in which events and interactions occur. It is above all an embodied and enacted process and considered a way of being in the world (Palmer and Hunter, 2018). Whilst I do not intend to be reflecting on worlding theory explicitly in the chapters, I do reveal a thread of implicit connections and certainly think that it is worth considering how individuals think and contextualise the TO they continue to have from early years to adulthood. Chapter 7, the final chapter, specifically aims to tackle and provoke further questions about some of these connecting and alternative lenses from cross-disciplinary viewpoints.

In this book the following chapters offer some introductory provocations for dialogue about being considered, reflected, and managed by those in authority within early childhood. It wrestles with a complex methodological understanding of practices within qualitative research and how policy and traditional discourses could be challenged. This is evident in specific examples such as the Teddy Bear Policy, celebrated in a school to support and redefine their positive behaviour policy.

It also aims to challenge thinking and questioning about the existence of the familiar approaches and provoke a review and reflect on the choices we make and the way we act and work, in offering opportunities and making connections with children in ways we perhaps hadn't previously considered. Throughout the book I hope to give examples that probe and create spaces for professionals working with children to initiate dialogues of practice that are challenging, are uncomfortable and extend alternative perspectives to notions of childhood and everyday practices with children (Hodgins, 2020).

Contextualising the Chapters

A broad range of themes are included in the chapter as the book navigates the reader toward specialist subjects and concepts. I have divided the book into two sections, initially exploring the theory and thinking about TO and childhood. The second part of the book moves towards thinking about TO and early years practice.

The Chapter Outlines

Chapter 1 – A Historical Overview of Sentimental Objects and Their Meanings in Transitions

Symbolic and sentimental objects from a historical perspective will introduce the chapter with a connection to early childhood. By exploring specific objects that hold sentimental and personal meanings, the reader is encouraged to reflect within and beyond their own personal experiences about emotions, play, relationships, and development. The chapter will also include the complexities towards sentimental objects from a parental perspective, including how an inanimate (non-human) object can become connected and identified as an extension of the young child as well as the adult. This will include the range of significant objects, including foundling tokens, symbolic objects found in the home (cabinet of curiosities) as well as the more traditional objects associated with children. These include objects such as dolls, cushions, and soothing items which have significant meaning both for the child and also the parent in their unfolding relationship. There will also be a discussion on capturing how the sentimental object moves back and forth as a Transitional Object (TO) or begins life as a TO and then becomes a sentimental object with its purpose and significance transformed. This will be extended to reflect on young children's personal objects, with a conceptual understanding about memory, materiality. Case study examples and reflective questions will be included throughout the chapter.

Chapter 2 – A Winnicott Partnership: The Winnicotts' Contributions to Psychoanalysis and Social Care

Focusing on 20th-century psychology, psychoanalysis, and social care work, both Donald and Clare Winnicott's contributions will be the prime foci for this chapter. It will explore and contextualise their own work and applications, developing their theories in relation to theory and practice. It will include the conceptual understanding of 'holding', referring to the supportive environment and caring relationships nurtured between young child and their primary carer. It will then introduce the transitional phenomena and the significance of TO. Throughout the chapter, examples will be given regarding the meanings TO have had with children.

Chapter 3 – Attachment, Object Relations, and Transitional Objects

Following on from the previous chapter, psychoanalysis and Winnicott's positionality will be extended, and this will move towards an examination about other key thinkers in this area, giving an introductory overview as well as a timeline in appreciating the engagement and distinction to each of them. Bowlby and attachment, with his theories about creating a secure base and separation anxiety will be included. Object Relations (OR) theory composed by Klein, Fairbairn and Winnicott will also be discussed. OR refers not to the inanimate objects but the significant others, who the child relates to. This is usually the primary carer as a whole person but can also be part of the person, such as the mother's breast. In developing a narrative about the concepts, there is the aim to emphasise the importance of nurturing young children. This should be within an encouraging and caring environment, with the child's needs met and their true self being able to emerge. This may lead on to Transitional Objects and these are introduced in relation to their value in the latter part of this chapter.

Chapter 4 – Transitional Objects: Parents, Personal to Public

This chapter will explore the primary carer and the experiences with their young children having Transitional Objects in the 21st century. It will further develop parenting approaches and cultural attitudes about 'chosen' TO in private and public spaces, from home to settings. Attention will be given to the value of TO within families and their purpose from the child's and parent's perspective. TO will be explored in relation to the importance of parent relationships and how humans and non-humans interact. The role of the professional is focused on and the areas reflected on regarding TO are the use of dummies, thumb sucking, and sleep time. The chapter will end with thinking about how working together in the parent–professional relationship can be achieved in the interest of the healthy development of the child.

Chapter 5 – Transitions and Formal Day Care

Transitional Objects will be explored in relation to young children. The chapter will further examine the psychological and potential space TO have to offer. It will also include the sense of trust and independence to be alone and play. Winnicott theorised that TO attachments and ego development lead to a sense of self. Additionally, the capacity for symbolisation, creativity, memory, empathy, and object relations are also weaved into the discussions. In drawing on empirical research, knowledge of TO will be further discussed, specifically their relevance in the 21st-century pandemic. Transitional times will be drawn on as examples to develop the discussion, offering TO as being purposefully relevant and serving a variety of psychological foundations as the child moves towards physical and emotional independence.

Chapter 6 – Transitional Objects in Early Years and Caring Contexts

This chapter will focus on the way Transitional Objects have been understood and accepted in formal day care, with reference to young children's emotional behaviour, health and hygiene and play, framed around setting policies. Practitioners' perspectives will be examined with their own understanding of the connections to transition objects, attachment, and security. Soft items and some personal objects were discouraged during the pandemic because of the concern about cross-contamination and complying with health and hygiene regulations. Subsequently the parents had to think about creative ways they could continue to support their young child during the transition to formal day care, and this included sewing a patch of their cuddle cloth to their inside jumper sleeve, or sterilising objects more frequently. Day care settings have also refused TO with a misunderstanding or misinformed understanding about the objects children bring in, some being a TO and other objects representing something else in the child's thinking. TO will therefore be explored in developing and widening the dialogue about their value to those working with young children, the way policy could be developed from the pandemic as well as ensuring the child remains at the heart of practice.

Chapter 7 – A Cross-Disciplinary Approach to Transitional Objects:
Symbolic, Transitional, and Sentimental Objects

This chapter explores the biography of symbolic, transitional, and sentimental objects and how objects can reveal understandings about individuals' past and present lives. This will be critically explored within differing contexts and by different professionals to widen the discussion about TO. The various and shifting ideas about objects being meaning makers and personalised will be discussed. The latter part of the chapter will then specifically focus on childhood and personal objects that have transitional meanings and a model that could be explored and discussed within formal day care settings.

Voice Vignettes and Questions Posed within the Chapters

Within each chapter voice vignettes are included to offer reflections and ideas for practice about the relevancy and how some of the themes presented could be shared as a community. By including these minutiae narratives, the lived experiences of having a TO are revealed. This includes voices from the past, as well as contemporary voices of professionals and children attending formal day care. The illustrative examples aim to complement the theory and questions are posed to further ignite and provoke thinking and discussion beyond the book.

Terms

Some of the terms included may seem culturally influenced, dated, or discordant with contemporary phrases, as well as perhaps offering a colloquial voice in describing an object. These have been included intentionally to ensure the authenticity of the voices and the way time shapes not only how we feel but also how we express ourselves. The word mother is interchanged with parent, and it is to be assumed that I use the word 'parenting' or 'caring' rather than 'mothering' as an inclusive word. Winnicott stressed the term mother in his writings and during the time it was accepted in what it aimed to convey. In 2023 the term mother may seem to disconnect the father or other carer in a parenting role, but this is not intentional. I have not sought to diminish other carers but rather to emphasise the role of the parent, and where I feel it is necessary to concur with Winnicott regarding the mother and her role with her child.

References

Anderson, B. and Harrison, P. (eds) (2010) *Taking-Place: Non-Representational Theories and Geography*. Farnham: Ashgate.
Haraway, D. (2008) *When Species Meet*. Minnesota: University of Minnesota Press.

Haraway, D. (2016) *Staying with the Trouble: Making Kin in the Chthulucene.* Durham, NC and London: Duke University Press.

Hodgins, H. (2020) *Feminist Research for 21st Century Childhood.* London: Bloomsbury.

Palmer, H. and Hunter, V. (2018) Worlding. *New Materialism.* Available at: https://newmaterialism.eu/almanac/w/worlding.html (accessed 14 April 2022).

Stewart, K. (2010) Worlding refrains. In M. Gregg and G. Seigworth (eds), *The Affect Theory Reader.* London: Duke University Press, 339–353.

Winnicott, D. W. (1953 [1951]) Transitional objects and transitional phenomena: A study of the first not-me possession. *International Journal of Psycho-Analysis,* 34: 89–97.

Part One

Transitional Objects and Early Childhood

Chapter 1

A Historical Overview of Sentimental Objects and Their Meanings in Transitions

Symbolic and sentimental objects from a historical perspective will introduce the chapter with a connection to early childhood. By exploring specific objects that hold sentimental and personal meanings, the reader is encouraged to reflect within and beyond their own personal experiences about emotions, play, relationships, and development. The chapter will also include the complexities towards sentimental objects from a parental perspective, including how an inanimate (non-human) object can become connected and identified as an extension of the young child as well as the adult. This will include the range of significant objects, such as foundling tokens, symbolic objects found in the home (cabinet of curiosities), as well as the more traditional objects associated with children. These include objects such as dolls, cushions, and soothing items which have significant meaning for both the child and also the parent in their unfolding relationship. There will also be a discussion about capturing how the sentimental object moves back and forth as a Transitional Object (TO) or begins life as a TO and then becomes a sentimental object with its purpose and significance transformed (see Figure 1.1). This will be extended by reflecting on young children's personal objects, with a conceptual understanding about memory, materiality. Case study examples, in the form of voice vignettes as well as reflective questions, will be included throughout the chapter.

A Material Culture: Living with Meaningful and Sentimental Non-humans

As professionals we recognise and are exposed, governed and responsive to numerous philosophies and theories about how we perceive and engage in our professional world as we work with young children from birth to five years in a range of formal day care settings. This can include policy adherence, national legislation, as well as the cultures we co-create in our daily work-place. However, to only conceive of this as purely dominated by human interactions and human relationships underestimates the non-human aspects of our everyday worlds. Traditionally, non-human entities are broadly defined as plants, animals, geology, and natural forces, as well as those things created

DOI: 10.4324/9781003296669-3

Figure 1.1 Transitional Objects come in many forms throughout the life span.

by humans such as art or music. Non-human can also be defined to include multiple entities within our understanding of 'things that are not human' and these can include natural phenomena, material structures, transportation devices, texts, and economic goods. We are therefore immersed in a world of humans, objects, and materials within our daily lived experiences (Hodgins, 2020).

Whilst this can feel an overwhelming way to think about the world, how we subjectively experience it affords wonderous and endless possibilities about how we can live ethically, re-conceptualising our position as early childhood professionals with the children in our care. In understanding this further, I have focused on how objects with an emotional attachment that provide transient security impact how children engage with their world and their worldly presence.

Whilst material culture is beyond the scope and direction of this chapter (and book) it would be appropriate to recognise the contributions to thinking about the non-human, material world around us, and how this influences our everyday life. Historically, women's relationship to material objects has been embodied in a connectivity of social and economic exchange rather than the often-conceived monetary exchanges found in society, governed and managed by males, from those in government to those in the family home. Often, we can categorise the products of women's skills in the form of the clothes made and worn, the contribution women have played in the textiles industry, and their cooking and gardening skills as part of family life. For women it was their invisible labour or non-paid employment that governed successful homes and ensured the survival of their children (McCarthy, 2020). Furthermore, the materiality of the past and present shapes and informs understanding about the way people lived and with such inventories illuminated the multiple connexions between the different domains in which women functioned.

Within female activities (as well as their male counterparts) the continual transformation of objects, the possessions retained, and commodities kept from one woman or household to another within the female world provide a rich and deeper understanding of lives connected with material goods, including their sentimental objects (Attfield, 2000). This again reminds me of The International Froebel Society Conference (2023) I attended and how a project presented amplified this area: Froebel and the 12th Gift – the occupation of sewing and how generational 'making' of sewing is not just a functional process of making something purposeful but also of being an emotive act, with timeless connections to relationships and non-human entanglements (Whinnett and Gill, 2023).

An area therefore less studied is the way the embodiment of material (matter and objects) shapes our emotions and sensory evaluations of our own experiences. From the taste of the food prepared and cooked to the feeling of clothing and the touch of a precious inherited hairbrush all invite our senses and connections to the material we engage in. The smell of our own and another's, for example, home and everyday spaces we immerse in, guide our constructions about who we are and how these can vary in social situations and in different cultures (Freeman, 2019).

Examples of Transitional Objects and Objects of Attachment: The Bunny

The 50-Year-Old Bunny Who Sits on the Mantel Piece and Was at One Time a TO

This was a gift from a relative. It used to have a long ribbon attached to its head and was used initially as a mobile toy on a pram. It was then used by the child and the ribbon was sucked and the ears stroked as they would settle to sleep. It is no longer a Transitional Object but rather a sentimental object similar to a prized ornament. It is a reminder of long-ago memories.

Objects with sentimental value in growing childhood are often treasured objects and among the first things we experience as valuable. In everyday life, we frequently experience seemingly sentimental value belonging to garments, books, cards, as well as larger objects such as buildings and geographical places. Sentiment in this example, is the emotion-involving relationships or experiences, connected to the object that is of value. Objects can take many forms and could even be a person's home. However although the house, as an object may have deep sentimental attachment it may also be entangled with financial costs and hardships for the owner in the desire to living there. Is the hardship and sacrifice of keeping the object, in this example the home, worth the pay-off?

Voice Vignette: The Sentimental House

This reminds me of the home of a family member. It is far too big and throughout the 40 years of residing there they have faced bankruptcy, limited holidays, and struggled to pay the bills. Children have moved away, yet the thought of moving is always met with absurdity and is a non-negotiable option. Even now, with the owners at 75 years, the heating is only on in a couple of the eight rooms. Measures have also been made (having lodgers) that ensure moving is unnecessary (anon, 2023).

Voice Vignette: Transitional Families

I can also relate to this when I recall a friend having to give up her canal boat, a boat she had lived on for years, prior to having a family, and then continued to use as central to her own family holidays. As an adult, her growing children did not want to return to the boat as often, seeking new experiences elsewhere. The final decision to sell the boat was the mother's. It was her boat and although in her programmatic way, she knew this made sense, financially and practically, her heart told her something else. She struggled to detach, with tears and emotions as the boat was sold and would share photographs and memories as she processed the transition from her boat. Of course, it was also the transition in her role as a mother, with her children detaching themselves from her as they grew older. She still often speaks about it. The boat was an object that was transitional and a secure base as she moved from adulthood, to independence, to wife, to mother.

A Sentimental Object?

Something is sentimentally valuable if and only if the thing is valuable for its own sake. It is also perhaps a subset of its relational properties, where the properties include any or all having belonged to, having been given to or by, or having been used by, people or animals, within a relationship of family, friendship, or romantic love, or having been used or acquired during a significant experience. For something to hold sentimental value it must have been used, for example, by someone with whom one is in a relationship that involves or involved largely positive sentiments, and they are the sentiments that give rise to the sentimental value. The sentiments that are necessary for the generation of sentimental value need not coexist with the value (Elmhirst, 1980).

Questions to Consider

- As a child, what home memories around your senses of smell, sight, touch do you recall?

- This may range from food cooked and tasted, the smell of curtains, a broken glass window or rough sleep mat. These objects shaped parts of your childhood as you and others engaged with them.
- Now consider any objects you still have or have replicated as an adult in your home life.
- Why these and what do they mean to you?

Therefore, objects have the capacity to unify individuals with each other as well as discriminating against others as they move and transition through their existence, engaging both with non-humans and humans. Objects also become the fragments of a larger association of people and things that is dependent on how we attach values to ourselves and to others (Edwards, 2006). The politics of representation and decolonising our understanding about material objects also has a part to play in early childhood.

Examples of Transitional Objects and Objects of Attachment: The Year-Long Christmas Decoration

I have a star hanging in my kitchen. It is a memory of an object I was given one Christmas, and now keep up all year as a reminder of that special time. It is not itself a TO but an object that represents the transitionary aspects of an annual cultural event, an event that brings a sense of belonging unity and connectedness within the family home.

Questions to Consider

- Are objects that are held dear by children representative of all children or only in specific cultures?
- Do early years professionals adopt a specific approach when reflecting on the relationship between children and objects and could these approaches be ethically considered within a care framework?

These are some of the questions discussed in the latter chapters but for now reflections and consideration to how objects matter to us is initially considered.

This is the idea that the body–mind can be regarded as enmeshed in the social trails created by the objects. For some individuals their physical movements between homes, towns, and countries occur with or in relation to the objects to which they attach themselves. Those humans forcibly displaced, such as refugees, for instance, often take what items they need for immediate practical use but also hold on to objects so they can either re-establish or redefine their subjective personal and collective origins. Mementoes of sentiment and cultural knowledge can therefore, according to Gibson (2004), provide the bases of future resettlement. The objects in transition, carried by individuals in crisis, can therefore offer the possibility of their own de-objectification and re-personalisation afterwards.

During the 20th century, Primo Levi's account of Auschwitz noted that many of those about to leave one camp to be taken to another, or an unknown destination, responded in a variety of ways, such as through prayer, or heavy drinking. However, the mothers, although in full knowledge of their fate, would continue to pack food and luggage as if they were going on a holiday. In the luggage their children's items would be included, such as toys and favourite cushions. They were conceived to be packing with emotion and tenderness to what effectively was a rite of passage to anticipatory mourning (Levi, 1987: 21–22). Similarly, the TO of childhood as identified by Winnicott (1953), discussed further in the next chapter, also acts as significant to the bereaved in adulthood. Individuals are often mourned through intimate things belonging to the deceased. It is not only the experience and process of grief that transitions with and through objects but objects themselves also transition in terms of their status, value, and meaning. Objects once intensely used in grieving are often experienced ambivalently later alongside the grieving process. As concrete symbolic materials, objects orient in time and space similarly to those relationships with children and objects in early childhood (Gibson, 2004).

Everyone feels vulnerable, insecure, or anxious at some point in their lives. During these times certain unique cherished objects can often hold a remarkable power to reassure us, to connect us to loved ones and to provide us with a sense of comfort and security. In a Memory Project of The Globe and Mail and the Dominion Institute, First World War artefacts were submitted. One of the most significant from nearly 3,000 objects was a tattered teddy bear, a treasured possession owned by a girl called Aileen Rogers. At the age of ten, she sent her bear in a care package to her father Lawrence who was working as a medic during the First World War. Lawrence treasured the bear, writing in a letter:

Tell Aileen I still have the Teddy Bear and I will try to hang on to it for her. It is dirty and his hind legs are kind of loose, but he is still with me.

When Lawrence was killed at Passchendaele in 1917, the bear, by then having lost both legs and eyes, was found with him and was returned home, later becoming one of the most significant artefacts in the Canadian War Museum (Bell and Spikins, 2018).

In exploring why, the story of the Rogers' bear is significant, as it reveals an insight into the powerful role of attachment objects in everyday lives. The emotional significance of the teddy bear highlights the connection humans have with objects and how they feel and respond to them when in their presence. It is the TO that can be moved with the child or adult as a source of comfort in the absence of the other close human.

In this example the bear became an attachment object to Lawrence, a source of comfort that he kept close to him until his death. Objects can therefore stimulate feelings related to positive, supportive and harmonious social relationships or affiliative emotions and feelings in several ways. Objects can also stimulate a nurturing response, and we can feel motivated to care for objects which are seen to be vulnerable or have been abandoned (Gorman and Wallis, 2017). Such objects can therefore provoke specific emotions related to the intense closeness we feel with our caregivers as a child and with close loved ones as adults in relationships in which we feel supported and cared for.

Another example is that of a contemporary programme being aired in England (2023), called *The Repair Shop*. Many of the people sending in the objects have a story about why they would like their object repaired, with some being TO. One example was a lady who, with her granddaughter, brought her doll in. It was a doll she had received from her father when he had returned from the Second World War. It was the first time she, as a four-year-old had seen her father, with the gift, the doll. The doll was described as the link to her father and as a child it supported her in her transitions and the connection to her father when he was absent. As a generational object the doll was something the granddaughter had also cherished, although perhaps for her it wasn't a transitional toy but was a link to her grandmother, and she would hold it and be comforted by it in her grandmother's absence. The programme repaired the doll, with new clothes and hair so it was transitioned back to how the 80-year-old grandma had seen it, for the first time, when she was four years old.

The 'Transitional Object' (Winnicott 1953) therefore prompted a sense of comfort and security like that of a caregiver but in its own right and providing a 'safe haven' and a 'secure base' to return to when the parent or carer is absent. Transitional Objects (TO), including teddy bears and blankets, can hold significance throughout adulthood, although other objects, even if perhaps not considered a TO, can perform a similar role as sources of the same feelings of comfort and security (Bell and Spikins, 2018).

Everyday Objects and Their Symbolic Representations and Meanings

As adults we often keep special objects as a reminder of our home. Objects such as gemstones are used as a symbolic reminder of our safe space. They are often placed in pockets and held for comfort as we enter and navigate unfamiliar places and spaces. Objects such as gemstones can therefore be our Talisman in working out and re-regulating our inner emotions, particularly in stressful situations.

Voice Vignette: My Rose Quartz

This chapter introduces the way we reflect about objects and their meanings in our lives. It also includes how the biography of objects can be symbolic in a child's everyday life. An object that has meaning for me is a rose gemstone.

The rose gemstone for me is the love I take with me to different places and different spaces. It moves with me, and I have had it for a long time. The rose gemstone moves from home to home. Whilst perhaps not a TO as defined by Winnicott, it still has value on an emotional level for me. I have it in my pocket and I feel it and stroke it in times of anxiety. The memories it holds are a reminder and, although through an adult lens, it's about what objects have in terms of meaning for us as individuals.

Question to Consider

• What objects do you have as you transition from spaces and places?

Exploring this further in childhood studies are considerations about entanglements and interaction, originally developed by Barad (2007) and adapted by Rautio (2013) within a post-humanist approach to childhood. For Barad it is concerned with interactional entanglements with others and the objects they have (Barad, 2007).

Voice Vignette: Listening and Observing Children and Their Objects

An example of this is a child named Jon. He has been attending a setting for a year, five days a week for about ten hours a day. As he prepared to go home from his setting, he would take some small world figures home and then return them to the setting. His parents took a photograph of his room, where he had lined up the figures on his television and named each one. He had named them after his peers at the setting and would change the figures periodically, with just two remaining the same and constant. For him it seemed that he wanted to take a part of the setting home with him as he settled in his home. He was an only child and often talked to them (Figure 1.2).

In Cortés-Morales (2021) study the author explored four children–mobilities–materialities entanglements ethnographically observed in Chile and the United Kingdom. Each of the case studies focused on a specific interaction between ordinary objects and children, other people, places, and the specific forms of movement originating or emanating from these entanglements. The first case study describes how a family maintained a connection at a distance through the aid of different but related forms of mobilities, with a focus on an iPad. The second was the story about a travelling object, in this case a pushchair. The unfolded and folded as aspects of the pushchair and its mobility is discussed whereby parents with young children rarely lack mobility aids. The pushchair is an extension of the walk, the object intertwined in the walk. The study also considered artefact or technology entanglement, mediating mobile relationships between children and adults travelling together, and between people and their mobile and spatial infrastructures, whether this is a car seat, a child leash, a baby carrier, a car, or a bus. The last two stories focused on

Figure 1.2 The small figures can represent family members of peers. The size of the figures is often welcomed, with children being able to fit them in their pocket and take them with them as they transition in spaces and places.

two entanglements involving bracelets, one of them in Santiago, Chile, and the other in a small English town. The bracelets, although very different in their materiality, value, treatment, and cultural significance, share a wearable quality that means the object moves with the person. As the stories unfold, other forms of movement and relationships emerge in relation to these two different bracelets, showing us the potential of this kind of materiality to reveal children's lives. For Lara, the bracelet, a birthday party present, remained with her, and she stayed focused on the bracelet and never stopped touching it until she fell asleep. The bracelet was not a permanent object in her everyday journeys or a key artefact that allowed her to be mobile. However, there was an instant and temporary physical and emotional attachment to the object. The bracelet connected Lara to her friend and his party – it allowed her to be part of that entanglement.

In developing a further insight into the significance of objects with sentimental value, shifting in and out of what Winnicott termed 'transitional objects', historical illustrations will highlight the complexity of the emotional attachment to objects.

Objects: Historical Objects and Their Retrospective Symbolic Representations and Meanings

An interesting and alternative perspective into objects is exploring how cabinets of curiosities became the aristocrat's answer during the Italian Renaissance. Collectors from the early 1600s used cabinets of curiosities to store and display rare and exotic objects such as medals, gems, or shells they had collected. The cabinets ranged in size, from as small as a dedicated piece of furniture, with multiple drawers, to the size of an entire room, the scale as mentioned earlier perhaps being indiscriminate to the emotions attached to the object/s?

Collecting precious objects had been a long-standing tradition among the elite classes, so early cabinets of curiosities regularly functioned as social status symbols. Drawers and shelves housed original objects acquired through long journeys to faraway lands. Every object in the cabinets of curiosities offered an opportunity to reveal a story about actual or imaginary travels. The objects in the cabinet therefore represented the owners' personal preferences and their personalities in the objects they collected. They therefore signified an illusion (or reality) of intelligence, wealth, and taste. The cabinets were a construction of their own personal versions of the world. Within the mini universe they created, the objects disclosed their deepest secrets, termed 'wonder rooms', and like today's museums, attempted to categorise and reveal stories about the natural world, beyond the everyday experiences (Mauries, 2019).

Objects as Emotional Tokens: The Baby Hat

The baby hat I kept was emotional because it was what an infant had worn when she was in a neonatal unit. She was quite poorly and with all the tubes and medical equipment the hat was something gifted from the mother. It was a special object and a reminder of the transition to motherhood, with all the anxieties and fear associated with it, as well as the celebrations of having transitioned successfully though it.

Ribbons in the 18th century were never simply a matter of the cloth from which garments were made. Accessorising was perceived as crucial to the clothing and no accessory was more versatile than ribbons which decorated women's heart sleeve gowns and the linen caps women wore. Vibrant colours and varied patterned ribbons signified romance, love, and courtship. Tying the ribbon into noughts that were known as love knots was defined by Samuel Johnson (1755, cited in Bright and Clark, 2014). Ribbons were also used to hang rings and tokens around the neck or tie them to another item or object of clothing for great intimacy. In the 18th century mothers commonly used the ribbons they attached to the babies' caps to distinguish between girls and boys, although they were not colour coded to identify the sex of the baby as is familiar today (Bright and Clark, 2014). It was not the colour of the ribbon sewn to the babies' cap that distinguished girls from boys, but the form of how the ribbon was attached. Girls' caps always took the form of what was called a top knot – a loose bunch of knotted ribbons with strands hanging down; ribbons attached to boys' caps, by contrast, were always in the form of a cockade and neatly formed a circular rosette.

Tokens were also used in the past to signify identity and arguably an emotional connection between mothers and their children. An example of this were the tokens used in identifying foundlings. In the 18th century, unimaginable destitution and poverty meant that many unmarried mothers faced abandoning their infants. When the Foundling Hospital was established, there was hope that these young babies and children, often abandoned in the streets, might survive. Furthermore, The Foundling Hospital made it possible for mothers to reclaim their babies if their circumstances changed. Therefore, each baby left was registered with a number and information to assist future identification. On the printed registration forms or 'billets', the gender of the child was noted, along with the clothes it was wearing, and any special distinguishing marks. In addition, the Hospital encouraged mothers to supply a 'token', which might be a note, or a small object, to be kept as an identifier so they could come back to collect their baby if their circumstances changed. They left coins, button, and scraps of ribbon (Bright and Clark, 2014). The most direct expressions of maternal emotion found among the tokens are those that showed a heart, by then a well-established symbol of love. Foundling mothers left 'hearts' playing cards, embroidered hearts, hearts cut out of fabric, and even, in the case of one baby boy, a gown printed with a hearts playing-card pattern (Stykes, 2019: 43).

The overwhelming majority of the tokens were little pieces of fabric, often with an accompanying letter or statement. They were kept in Coram's billet books as an identifying record for more than 4,000 babies handed to the Hospital between 1741 and 1760, attached to registration forms (Berry, 2019).

The Coram Story (2019) describes the power of these humble objects:

> The textiles are both beautiful and poignant, embedded in a rich social history. Each swatch reflects the life of a single infant child. But the textiles also tell us about the clothes their mothers wore, because baby clothes were usually made up from worn-out adult clothing. The fabrics reveal how working women struggled to be fashionable in the 18th century.

Objects: Childhood Personal and Sentimental Objects

Voice Vignette: Teddy

This was a bear given to a lady who is now in her late seventies. She tells the story of how Edward Bear was given to her by her father when she was one year old,

> I have still got him. I think that all the drawn claws on the limbs have a smile. I love him and he is a place of comfort. I use two of the senses, touch, and smell when I hold him. Edward Bear is now 73 years old, and I have got photos of me with him when my first child was born. He is now 53 years old.

Figure 1.3 Edward Bear.

In capturing how important the bear is to her, she personifies his life.

> Ted
> I am Ted.
> 73-years-old Ted,
> A once cuddly Ted,
> Communicating and connecting with my human
> I have lived in age, and I am old now, but I still feel loved.
> I am an experienced Ted.
> A living memory of everlasting cuddles with my human.

According to Brenner (cited in Goddard, 2014; Brenner et al., 2021), significant objects with an emotional attachment continue through the course of our lives. As sacred keepsakes they can allow us to return to and reflect on a place and time of great comfort and a memory. The identification, and attachment to objects outside of the self, can include photographs, wedding bands, mementos, music, art, and culture, which not only define nostalgic memorials, but also ensure a secure base in making the connection and presence in the world, from our past to our present.

Studies of the meanings that certain objects hold for their owner across the lifespan suggest that inanimate objects embody a multitude of meanings and functions that are significant for adults as well as children. They suggest the objects often symbolise social bonds and emotional memories (Kamptner, 1995).

Clinical studies of adults' use of TO also reported that certain objects come to function as physical embodiments of a significant person, and that physically touching or seeing that object strengthens the owner's own awareness of the other person. By emotionally reflecting they are able to emotionally hold that person in their mind when they are separated (Arthern and Madill, 1999). The object becomes an emotional connection to the other person with feelings of love, comfort, and emotional closeness experienced. The object can also reduce the anxiety of separation from both those in the here and now as well as those that are no longer living. The objects in childhood continue to be significant emotionally and physically and this is often apparent with the loss of the object.

An example of this is by Philo (2018), 'When Teddy met Teddy'. It is the recollection of a lost teddy and how the teddy signifies loss as well as its significance in the child's geographies of life during transitional times.

> Teddy I no longer live with Teddy. He decided to stay at my parents' house when I went to university, probably because he is a creature of haunts and habits. Teddy – for that is his unimaginative name – was not my original teddy, and he always struggled to fill the role vacated by his predecessor, also called Teddy, who was left on a train when I was very young. Original Teddy, even now, possibly retains a higher place in my affections than replacement Teddy: the former really was my most crucial 'transitional object' as I grew from 'crib geographies' (Aitken and Herman 1997) into the bedroom geographies of a small boy. Replacement Teddy was nonetheless a significant actor in the context of my micro-world-making from circa 4 to circa 12 years of age. Unlike original Teddy, he almost never accompanied me, being very much a stay-at-home bear rather than constant travelling companion. Typically, he inhabited my bedroom, sometimes sitting on my bed but more normally standing on a shelf, where he increasingly spent his days as I grew into my teens, the call to be involved in my activities becoming ever rarer. Indeed, he saw me less and less as my bedroom ceased to be a site of sustained encounter and more a functional site of sleep, clothes-changing and homework. It mattered to me that he was there, however, and it matters, not massively but in a small way, that he remains there still, on the same shelf in the same room in the same house (pp. 1–2).

Sarner (2018) extends this by considering the psychological power of toys throughout life and illustrates this again with adults recollecting their feelings around their toys. An example of this is Chris who had a piece of blue cloth when he was four years old. He kept it with him and named it Boo-Boo. As a retired teacher of 60 years, a husband and father of three adult children, he still remembers the emotional connection and feelings of safety when he would gently rub the soft fabric against his face or between his fingers.

The British artist Grayson Perry is also inspired by his 60-year-old childhood teddy bear called Alan Measles, within his artwork. He refers to his teddy as magical – his talismanic teddy.

He named his teddy after contracting measles as a three-year-old. He considers Alan Measles, his teddy, as the benign dictator of his imaginary world from about the age of four up to 14 years of age. In moving towards self-sufficiency Alan played a central role, replacing his troubled relationship with his stepdad. Grayson Perry has since featured his bear, Alan Measles, in much of his art, and has written that the bear also accompanied him round Europe in a glass shrine. This is an illustration about how many of us have keepsakes and objects that we find solace in – they bring good luck and have mystical powers, accompanying us in our journey of life. For Perry, the threadbare Alan continues to play an important role in his life from childhood through to adulthood, being created in many forms, and in differing materials from metal to ceramic versions of him (BeMyBear, 2019).

Similarly, Jones, at age 45 years, still has her teddy which was gifted during her first year of primary school as well as Robertson, who at 50 years still remembers clinging to his panda, even when his brother chewed one of his panda's eyes out. Panda, in the present, occupies the best chair in his house. Graham, another example of having a teddy in his youth, still talks to his Ted and sits on a bookcase near his chair (Sarner, 2018).

These examples highlight how TO continue to have meaning throughout life, although emphasis is often placed in the early years. Perhaps, as we argue, they transition to being sentimental objects, symbolising a time and place, differentiated from what Winnicott terms TO.

Another adult reminisces about how her doll evokes memories that have significance. She recalls how her mum was working so hard, and late, but still found time and space to think about her child on her way home. As an adult, the older you get, the more meaningful these objects become in a different way. It is in a sense contextualised back to a time and place that perhaps mirrors another generation, the object being the constant between the generations.

However, some studies have indicated that whilst having a TO is considered normal, there is a distinction that being unable to let go of a TO, as defined by Winnicott, into adolescent and adult years can be indicative of problems such as high stress, low self-esteem, coping with stress, trauma, or difficult situations (Erkolahti et al., 2016). Little is known about the continuation of TO use into adolescence, and fewer studies have been conducted with non-Western populations. In the study by Stagg and Li (2019), they examined the differences in attachment and attitudes of adolescents who used a TO. Some 723 adolescents from Taiwan (mean age 14 years) were asked about their current and past use of TO. Thirty-seven per cent of the sample were found to have continued TO use in adolescence. They also found TO users were less likely to have secure attachments and less likely to express positive attitudes towards seeking help. Whilst this was a small-scale study and cannot be generalised, it does offer some further questions about how objects can be used as a buffer against anxiety and in part evaluate forms of support a young adult may need (Stagg and Li, 2019). Researchers have also found that girls were more likely to have a TO than boys and that the types of TO that girls and boys typically have differ, mostly on account of what types of toys are typically given to boys and girls based on gender norms (Erkolahti and Nyström, 2009).

Girls were more likely to have soft to touch TO like blankets and stuffed animals, and boys more likely to have hard to touch TO like action figures and toy cars. However, there is no consensus on whether attachment to material objects during adulthood is the norm or a sign of problems during adulthood (Hooley and Wilson-Murphy, 2012; Winnicott, 1953). Across cultures, a study conducted by Stagg and Li (2019) revealed that Taiwanese children were more likely to have TO than American children. This cultural difference is attributed to differences in child rearing practices as well as different school systems. The Taiwanese children in the study had less access to quality education with support systems than the American children had. Therefore, Taiwenese children with less support systems were arguably more likely to have TO later into their adolescence (Stagg and Li, 2019).

Furthermore, Wapner, Demick, and Redondo (1990) studied elderly people in nursing homes and found that attachment to objects helped them to cope with and regulate their emotions, but this was not determined by specific behaviour of the elderly population. Research by the University of Amsterdam (2013) found that cuddling a teddy can lower stress levels and help come to terms with mortality.

With reference to young adults, a third of students were found to take their ted to university. This was for various reasons, including help overcoming the separation from families, loneliness, homesickness, and changing lifestyles. Philippa Perry (2014) confirms just because adults have other ways of dealing with life's conflicts, it doesn't necessarily mean the relinquishment of much-loved bears and personal toys from childhood.

Winnicott also stated that the task of accepting external reality is never completed and that no human is completely free from the tension of relating their inner and outer realities. It is therefore arguably realistic to assume there is sanctuary and comfort in personal objects. Transitional Objects are therefore psychologically beneficial for young children. A TO that is textually soft may further contribute to creating positive relational emotions as studies have found that, regardless of age, touching or holding soft objects is comforting, stress-reducing, and calming. The act of touching soft things may also release opioids in the brain, and therefore increase oxytocin levels to induce positive emotions, and reduce the stress hormone cortisol (Norman, 2019).

Objects: The Emotional Significance of Objects in Early Childhood

In consideration of young children and their relationship with objects, I turn to initially considering their emotional processes more broadly, and in relation to the humans and non-humans in their world.

It is particularly important for babies to learn about the people who nurture, protect and take care of them, who love them and figure out that love works. All children want and need love for protection and nurturance. This is considered innate and universal and a necessary part of the evolutionary scheme of protected maturity. However, care can take many different forms and baby's concepts about love can significantly vary. After about a year, affectionate trust becomes centred on a few familiar people, not just those very close to them. They may also become anxious when strangers approach and engage (Gopnik, 2016).

Children therefore may need us to co-regulate their emotions as it might be difficult to make choices when they are overwhelmed. An offer of emotional support can be met through self-selected objects and symbols as well. When relationships are built on trust in which children and adults respect the emotions and feelings of others, this leads to a more democratic, humane, and cohesive relationship. From birth, babies are surrounded by fabrics, their first swaddling cloth, hats, and clothes. In many cultures, these first materials are chosen with care by parents and carers and offered in naming ceremonies (Winnicott, 2016). Babies explore fabrics with their whole bodies and particularly their fingers, mouths, and cheeks. These objects can be a source of emotional support. The object allows for and invites emotional well-being, and without such an object, true feelings may be concealed, suppressed, or dismissed as the infant/child has no other means by which to cope with, comprehend, and contend with the world. In contemplating my own pedagogical influences, I consider myself a Froebelian thinker. I am drawn to the ways Froebel conceptualises how children express and process their feelings in various ways. Froebel introduced the concept of making the 'inner outer' and the 'outer inner'. Inner knowledge, thoughts, and feelings are expressed outwardly through behaviours and demonstrated through outer activity and experiences, such as the relationship with humans and non-humans (McNair and Cerdan, 2022).

Voice Vignette: The Inner and Outer

Graham is a retired nurse who lives with his wife and object, Ted. Although Ted faded into the background of Graham's life as he grew older, his significance has never waned and reasserts itself at times of distress. 'I was very upset. I packed a suitcase – it wasn't even full – and I packed him. I didn't get the rest of my belongings for months. But he was a part of me, and it was important that I didn't lose him,' he says. For him Ted still represented stability and durability (Sarner, 2018).

These objects can be a source of emotional support. The object allows for and invites emotional well-being.

Question to Consider

- Can you recall what objects have provide you with emotional support and well-being?

Voice Vignette: Fractured Memories and Self-Editing Memories on Play and the Objects of My Own Past within My Play

I remember the emotionally charged juxtaposed position I was in when I was about seven years old. Conscious stream of thoughts occurring about how I should play, what way should I play, and ultimately feeling too 'old' to play. I recall feeling uncomfortable and visibly looking at peers during school – did they still play dolls at home? Did they make believe? Today I can appreciate that play comes in many forms and genres and being playful can also form part of a play experience. So, from this perspective I think my epiphany moment (Denzin, 2022) was an awareness of the shift from a specific from of play, playing with toys and being immersed in playing with them that I felt I was moving beyond, whilst wanting to hold onto specific objects as I transitioned from spaces.

Whilst seven years old seems rather specific and perhaps, arguably, a memory later recalled rather than a conscious thought occurring at the time, it is an interpretation I perceive as my reality. I can metaphorically transport myself back to the school year, the teacher, the playground, and the observations of peers around me. I recall the provoked thought of play and feeling too old to play was a result of a casual conversation in the playground about a television programme of the time. During the early 1980s in England there was a teatime slot of programmes for younger children and then later programmes for a slightly older audience, although I continued to enjoy Playschool, a programme for a younger audience, with crafts, and songs even, and would also watch it regularly. The presenters relied on soft toys, teddies, dolls, and plush toys. During this time there were limited channels to watch, and television was still a novelty for many children. In addition, I was not allowed to watch the programmes aimed at older children, so my shift in outgrowing certain programmes was from the content rather than linked to popularity.

Home Life: A Playful Time

So, what did I recall playing as a young child during my cultural upbringing? I remember vividly having a chalk board with a purpose and task set. If I had teddies, dolls, or any other soft toy they would be sat facing me so I could sit and instruct them, sharing my experiences of the school day. This directed play and symbolic form of play mirrored my personal life of the time. I look back and realise the control I desired, the safe structure of the teacher–child relationship at school, and the manipulation to alter the outcome of the teaching with my toys were valuable to me. What I do not recall was the cuddling, the emotional warmth, the needing of my toys, in a cuddly and physical way. Rather I was the leader of them and had control.

The turning point, my epiphany moment, in bringing together a conscious thought about play and the TO within it was at the age when family life consumed my reality.

During this year I had a brother and sister and two parents. However, in the January after my mother's pregnancy-related illness, my family was extended with the arrival of a new baby sister. This transition was carried over a few months and catapulted me into 'older' sibling. My memory of this time was cuddling, petting, and rocking her daily. I discarded the blackboard and chalks that I had carried to and fro from my grandmother's when I lived there temporarily – it had been a compulsive need to retain them in a bag and then play teacher and direct a select few toys.

Living in a guest house my family often entailed a number of additional people living under one roof and my mother spending most days cleaning, organising, and nipping in to feed my sister and then busying off again. Therefore, this allowed me the time to feel responsible, caring, and nurturing to a real human. For me she was the ultimate prize doll. The doll little children, both girls and in some cases if allowed, boys, have so they can pet, brush their hair, dress and generally fuss over, was for me replaced with a real live infant. What could be better? I was given responsibility to be careful, to hold her in a certain way, to change her and to talk to her. She became the object I had desired. As she grew, my attention to her did not diminish and rather intensified as she was weaned and later fed from a bottle. I was confident in that she would not break if I changed her and whilst my older brother of two years and younger sister of three years were mildly interested, I was almost suffocating her with love and attention from morning to night. The only respite I or she had was during school hours where I was expected to resume my role as child, feeling and thinking like a child of eight. This was perhaps exasperated in the summer of that year with the passing of a close Grandma, a key matriarchal figure of the family, my mother's mother. She had cared for us whilst my mother had been ill in late pregnancy and although elderly herself was a retired teacher with a clarity of ways how to do things and how to be.

Play Imitating Life

So, my play and understanding about my play objects and or TO of the blackboard during this time shifted. Was it because of my personal exposure to mortality and longevity of life? Was it recognition of the responsibility and preciousness of a new-born and the vulnerability of the elderly through illness? My play certainly reflected a form of control, a teacher with a narrow vision, completing the task, marking the books, and playing with the chalk board to ensure understanding was achieved. Perhaps this style of play was influenced by my grandma's professional life and character constructed from many years as a teacher. Probably.

Was I given a choice to opt in and out of child care and be a child, maybe? My memories are filled with a wanting and desire to care for my sister, to talk to her, and to love her. Perhaps this was too much for a eight-year-old. Perhaps knowing she was being watched and attended to satisfy my mother's own guilt of not spending time with her when trying to manage the household when my father was away at work. I am sure a mixture of all this contributed to my stark and abrupt feelings of how I played ... in that playground, on that day, talking to my peers about what programmes we liked.

Shaping of My Life and Life's Work

So, I reflect and think about how these earlier experiences of play and life influence my adult self and shape who I am today? My play was my reality, my family life growing up. After my sister came another brother when I was eleven years of age and being one of five in a family. My closeness to my family was therefore compounded and whilst family was rocky and tense, my own nurturing feelings grew and developed. My understanding of doll play became child care and, as I grew and matured, I could communicate with my mother about her feelings as a parent and her starkly different upbringing. An existence of 1950s English boarding schools as an only child created a reactionary life trajectory of ensuring she was never alone as an adult. For me it was about understanding those formative years and studying why infants behave the way they do, training as a teacher and play therapist. It made me reflect on the ways children perceive their play and how as a result I was given so much real-life freedom that I was unable to play out and try alternative existences.

Winnicott says TO are more than comfort and that they lead to play, fundamental to the development of a healthy mind. The TO is defined as 'the first "not me" possession', but often the boundary between the self and the other remains fluid as they grow and develop (Winnicott, 1953). In Winnicott's theory, these possessions are about more than comfort and they lead to play, which is fundamental to the development of a healthy mind. In what he calls 'the intermediate space' that opens between mother and baby, occupied and stretched by the TO, the child's imagination and creativity grow. Playing is a therapy.

Questions to Consider

- What are your experiences of play in childhood?
- Has play shaped your thinking from a post human perspective?

Objects: The Object and the Transitional Space of Early Childhood in Defining Transitional Objects

Linus's security blanket made its first appearance in *Peanuts* in 1954, three years after the paediatrician and psychoanalyst Donald Winnicott wrote his seminal paper on Transitional Objects (TO). He would later ask Schulz for permission to use Linus's blanket as an illustration of his theory.

The transition in Winnicott's TO refers to the shift every infant must make, as he wrote,

> from a state of being merged with the mother to a state of being in relation to the mother as something outside and separate.
>
> (Winnicott, 1971: 14–15)

Angela Joyce, the chair of the Winnicott Trust and a fellow of the British Psychoanalytical Society, explains that, for Winnicott: The baby is merged with the mother, as one. As the infant to child develops, their body, memory, and interests in the objects and the people around them mature, with many selecting something that becomes special and used during periods of separation.

A TO therefore tends to be chosen in the first six months of life and to have qualities reminiscent of the mother. They are often, but not always, soft and can be stroked, cuddled, and bitten. At a symbolic level, the TO links to maternal care, aiding the feeling of loss when the mother is absent. These object attachments decrease distress and anxiety while providing comfort and security for young children during separations from the parent. As a representation of the bond with the mother, the TO was conceived as a "bridge" between the child's inner world, including the attachment bond and the outer world, for example, the reality of having to cope with separations from her. TO may therefore be especially helpful to parents who must endure separations from their young children. Having a special object to touch, see, and hold can be a visual and physical reminder of, and an emotional connection to, a young child (Hughes and Baylin (2012), cited in Kamptner, 2019).

A Final Note

This chapter has grappled with the ideas around objects, the longevity of objects that have emotional significance and the acknowledgement of Winnicott's TO. It has included a range of vignettes and the aim is to be able to reflect on our own positions as adults about the non-human objects in our life so we have a better understanding about how to support the children we care for.

References

Arthern, J. and Madill, A. (1999) How do transitional objects work? The therapist's view. *British Journal of Medical Psychology*, 72 (1): 1–21. https://doi.org/10.1348/000711299159754

Attfield, J. (2000) *Wild Things: The Material Culture of Everyday Life*. Oxford: Berg Publishers.

Barad, K. (2007) *Meeting the Universe Halfway: Quantum Physics and the Entanglement of Matter and Meaning*. Durham: Duke University Press.

Bell, T. and Spikins, P. (2018) The object of my affection: Attachment security and material culture. *Time and Mind*, 11 (1): 23–39. https://doi.org/10.1080/1751696X.2018.1433355

BeMyBear (2019) We're never too old to go to bed with a teddy bear – and that's official! (blog). Available at: www.bemybear.com/blog/were-never-too-old-to-go-to-bed-with-a-teddy-bear-and-thats-official

Berry, H. (2019) *Orphans of the Empire*. Oxford: Oxford University Press.

Brenner, I., Bachner-Melman, R., Lev-Ari, L., Levi-Ogolnic, M., Tolmacz, R., and Ben-Amitay, G. (2021). Attachment, sense of entitlement in romantic relationships, and sexual revictimization among adult CSA survivors. *Journal of Interpersonal Violence*, 36 (19–20). https://doi.org/10.1177/0886260519875558

Bright, J. and Clark, G. (2014) *Tokens at The Foundling*. London: Foundling Museum.

Coram Story (2019) The Foundling Hospital tokens collection. Available at: https://coramstory.org.uk (accessed October 14, 2021).

Cortés-Morales, S. (2021) Bracelets around their wrists, bracelets around their worlds: Materiality's and mobilities in (researching) young children's lives. *Children's Geographies*, 19 (3): 364–376. https://doi.org/10.1080/14733285.2020.1789559

Denzin, N. K. (2022) Scenes from masked and anonymous. *Qualitative Inquiry*, 28 (10): 1101–1103. https://doi.org/10.1177/10778004221080786

Edwards, E. (2006) *Sensible Objects: Colonialism, Museums and Material Culture*. Wenner-Gren International Symposium Series. Oxford: Berg Publishers.

Elmhirst, S. I. (1980) Transitional objects in transition. *The International Journal of Psychoanalysis*, 61 (3): 367–373.

Erkolahti, R. and Nyström, M. (2009) The prevalence of transitional object use in adolescence: Is there a connection between the existence of a transitional object and depressive symptoms? *European Child & Adolescent Psychiatry*, 18 (7): 400–406. https://doi.org/10.1007/s00787-009-0747-7

Erkolahti, R., Nyström, M., Vahlberg, T., and Ebeling, H. (2016) Transitional object use in adolescence: A developmental phenomenon or a sign of problems. *Nordic Journal of Psychiatry*, 70 (7), 536–541, https://doi.org/10.1080/08039488.2016.1179339

Freeman, C. (2019) Twenty-five years of children's geographies: A planner's perspective. *Children's Geographies*, 18 (1): 110–121. https://doi.org/10.1080/14733285.2019.1598547

Gibson, M. (2004) Melancholy objects. *Mortality*, 9 (4): 285–299. https://doi.org/10.1080/13576270412331329812

Goddard, C. (2014) More than just teddy bears: Transitional objects allow a child's inherent sense of self to emerge. *Psychology Today*. Available at: www.psychologytoday.com/gb/blog/the-guest-room/201407/more-just-teddy-bears.

Gopnik, A. (2016) *The Gardener and the Carpenter: What the New Science of Child Development Tells Us about the Relationship between Parents and Children*. New York: Farrar, Straus & Giroux.

Gorman, A. and Wallis, L. (2017) *Loveable: The Stories behind Thriftshop Objects*. Brighton, SA: Wallis Heritage Consulting.

Hodgins, H. (2020) *Feminist Research for 21st-century Childhood*. London: Bloomsbury.

Hooley, J. M. and Wilson-Murphy, M. (2012) Adult attachment to transitional objects and borderline personality disorder. *Journal of Personality Disorders*, 26 (2): 179–191.

Kamptner, L. (2019) Transitional objects: Helpful for parents too? *CuddleBright*. Available at: www.cuddlebright.com/learn/transitional-objects-helpful-for-parents-too

Kamptner, N. L. (1995) Treasured possessions and their meanings in adolescent males and females. *Adolescence*, 30 (118): 301–318.

Levi, P. (1987 [1958]) *If This Is a Man*. London: Abacus, Sphere Books.

Mauries, P. (2019) *Cabinets of Curiosities*. London: Thames & Hudson.

McCarthy, H. (2020) *Double Lives*. London: Bloomsbury.

McNair, L. and Cerdan, C. (2022) Nurturing self-regulation. Frobel Pamphlet. Available at: www.froebel.org.uk/news/new-pamphlet-nurturing-self-regulation

Norman, A. (2019) *From Conception to Two*. London: Routledge.

Perry, P. (2014) Teddy bears for adults: Why a third of students take a teddy bear with them to university. *The Independent*, September 29. Available at: www.independent.co.uk/life-style/health-and-families/features/teddy-bears-for-adults-why-a-third-of-students-take-a-teddy-bear-with-them-to-university-9763494.html

Philo, C. (2018) When teddy met teddie. *Children's Geographies*, 16 (4): 455–458. https://doi.org/10.1080/14733285.2018.1457754

Rautio, P. (2013) Children who carry stones in their pockets: On autotelic material practices in everyday life. *Children's Geographies*, 11 (4): 394–408.

Sarner, M. (2018) Still have your childhood teddy? The psychological power of the toys we keep. *The Guardian*, December 12. Available at: www.theguardian.com/society/2018/dec/12/still-have-childhood-teddy-psychological-power-toys-we-keep (accessed September 28, 2023).

Stagg, S. and Li, Y. C. (2019) Transitional object use, attachment and help seeking behaviour in Taiwanese adolescents. *Asian Journal of Social Psychology*, 22 (2), 163–171.

Styles, J. (2010) Threads of Feeling. Foundling Museum. Available at: https://foundlingmuseum.org.uk/events/threads-of-feeling/ (accessed September 30, 2020).

University of Amsterdam (2013) in BeMyBear (2019) We're never too old to go to bed with a teddy bear – and that's official! Available at: bemybear.com (accessed October 11, 2023).

Wapner, S., Demick, J. and Redondo, J. P. (1990) Cherished possessions and adaptation of older people to nursing homes. *The International Journal of Aging and Human Development*, 31 (3): 219–235. https://doi.org/10.2190/GJPL-ATJY-KJA3-8C99

Whinnett, J. and Gill, C. (2023) *Stitching*. The International Froebel Society Conference, Maynooth, Ireland.

Winnicott, D. W. (1953) Transitional objects and transitional phenomena. A study of the first not-me possession. *International Journal of Psychoanalysis*, 34: 89–97. https://doi.org/10.1093/med:psych/9780190271350.001.0001

Winnicott, D. W. (1971) *Playing and Reality.* New York: Basic Books.

Winnicott, D. W. (2016) Transitional objects and transitional phenomena. In L. Caldwell and H. Taylor (eds), *The Collected Works of D. W. Winnicott: Volume 9, 1969–1971.* New York: Oxford Academic. Available at: https://doi.org/10.1093/med:psych/9780190271411.003.0052 (accessed June 4, 2023).

Chapter 2

A Winnicott Partnership

The Winnicotts' Contributions to Psychoanalysis and Social Care

Focusing on 20th-century psychology, psychoanalysis, and social care work, both Donald and Clare Winnicott's contributions will be the prime foci for this chapter. It will explore and contextualise their own work and applications, developing their theories in relation to theory and practice. It will include the conceptual understanding of 'holding', referring to the supportive environment and caring relationships nurtured between young child and their primary carer. It will then introduce the transitional phenomena and the significance of Transitional Objects (TO). Throughout the chapter examples will be given regarding the meanings TO have had with children.

The Biography to Developing an Understanding about the Theory

Initially, it is worth making sense of the journey taken and the desire of wanting to focus specifically on TO and their relevance within formal day care. The inspiration came from reflecting about the way practitioners viewed TO, at how their views about them were at odds on several occasions with the psychotherapists and play therapists clinically working with children. This was compounded by the pandemic from 2020 when the English government produced a safe working document and within it there was the discouragement of soft toys and objects being allowed in settings for fear that cross-contamination of the virus would occur. This led to my own questioning about what and how we think about objects and their place in a child's world. From a post humanist perspective, of course they are as important as the humans and this further caused entanglements in my thinking about what messages we convey and how much we authentically listen to the child, our behaviour directed by nationally imposed policies within the national early years curriculum. In resisting or complying with these forces where does the child's agency fit in all of this? This led me to wanting to pursue how a therapeutic approach could be embraced in a variety of places and spaces in early years. In meeting with generous and compassionate members of the Squiggle Trust I have been fortunate to continue this journey and share an introductory

DOI: 10.4324/9781003296669-4

insight into Winnicott that will ignite further reading and understanding about early childhood and their first 'not me' possessions. So, what does the Squiggle Trust set out to do?

The Squiggle Foundation's aims are:

- To study the work of Donald Winnicott (1896–1971).
- To spread his ideas to a wide audience and put them into everyday use in today's world.

Where does the word squiggle come from? The word 'squiggle' comes from a method Winnicott used to facilitate communication with a child. He would take turns with the child to make a small squiggle mark on a sheet of paper and each would then extend the other's squiggle into a simple drawing of personal significance. Playing with a scribble drawing was one way in which Winnicott led the child to a better sense of self. His writings revolve around three main issues:

- The mother–infant relationship.
- Transitional phenomena, most clearly recognised in a child's intense possessive feelings for a special blanket or toy.
- The importance of play and primary creativity (Candlin and Guins, 2009).

Who Is Winnicott?

Winnicott was a paediatrician and psychoanalyst who built on Freud's (1905a) discoveries about the mind and the internal and external forces that influence it. Winnicott's main emphasis was on the authentic flourishing of the 'person' and the nurturing by the 'other' of a 'sense of self'. Winnicott's concerns were with holistic living persons, and loving. His clinical/therapeutic aim was to enable his patients to be able to live in a creative and authentic way (Horne and Lanyado, 2012). This definition of Winnicott, I suspect resonates with many early years professionals and the way they would support, nurture, and love a child though compassionate care.

Winnicott is frequently known as the psychologist who developed the thinking around objects and their emotional value, Transitional Objects. With transition, Winnicott means an intermediate development area between the psychic and external reality. It is then that we can find the TO, which is the first element leading the child to face the external reality, through the creation of symbols. To understand this further, attachment and emotional connections to objects and humans need to be considered.

It is also a reminder of Harry Harlow's earlier experiments with infant monkeys and how their fear was reduced when in the presence of an inanimate cloth surrogate 'mother' (Harlow and Zimmermann, 1959). The attachment to an object with children can therefore be thought of as establishing a protective factor with the presence of the object granting the child a sense of protection (Rutter, 1985, cited in Fortuna et al., 2014). Harlow, Dodsworth, and Harlow (1965) discovered that when given the choice between a soft surrogate mother and a hard wire mesh offering food and water, the monkeys would feed from the wire mother but then chose to spend their time with the soft surrogate mother rather than be near the food and the wire mother. Harlow et al.'s study findings focused on the innate desire for comfort, which is seen in these monkeys as well as humans. Bowlby (1969) also posited that people are born with an innate desire to form attachments to people and things around them. The primary source of attachments for a child would be the child's parents or close and emotionally present guardians. An individual's attachment style is formed during childhood based on whether their attachment needs are met. A child would form a secure attachment style if their needs were met, and would form anxious, avoidant, or disorganised attachment styles if their needs were not met (Norman, 2019).

In the mid-20th century theories of child development were predominantly influenced by experiences of the war in England, with family breakdowns, separation and evacuation being part of the fabric to a child life (Fortuna et al., 2014). Similarly, Donald Winnicott was the youngest child, and his recollections of his childhood and early experience were shrouded with mental health problems. From this experience he wanted to help other people troubled with psychological problems. Winnicott studied medicine at Jesus College in Cambridge in 1914 and joined the Royal Navy in 1917. He completed his medical degree at the University of London's St. Bartholomew's Hospital Medical College. In 1923, Winnicott began working as a paediatrician at the Paddington Green Children's Hospital, where he remained until 1962. Winnicott then developed an interest in psychoanalysis, and he studied under Melanie Klein, a highly influential and revered psychoanalyst (Mason, 2003). She refuted many of Freud's theories on child development and developed her own thinking about infant development and the psyche, being further discussed in the subsequent chapter. It is important to note at this stage though that it was these influences that shaped Winnicott and his professional work, becoming a child analyst in 1935 and then a full member of the British Psychoanalytic Society in 1936 (Caldwell, 2007).

During his professional career as he met children and theorised about childhood, Winnicott distanced himself from Klein's work and developed his own theories on child development. He developed several theories and concepts that helped shape the way in which psychoanalysis is practised today.

Her Story: Clare Winnicott's Contribution

Whilst we often hear of Donald Winnicott, it would be a disservice to not include his partner and wife, Clare Winnicott who was a significant figure in developing his theory. It was her work and connection to families that bridged theory with everyday practice.

Claire Winnicott was a social worker and made invaluable contributions after the Second World War. During the 1950s she recognised the mental health concerns of parents and their infants as well as the support that was needed for them to move forward to achieve good health and well-being. This included much smaller organised accommodation for those in need and the use of psychiatric social workers with specialised skills that could support the parents. Significant about Clare was her understanding to the importance in contacting and talking with parents when their children had been separated. Clare's observations of TO during the war were also significant in understanding her contribution to the theory. Claire travelled to London to seek out the parents of the children in hotels and hostels as she considered some knowledge of their family would be central to their own and their children's emotional development. When she found the parents, she asked them to prepare a note or give them something to take to the children. To maintain satisfactory relationships with their children, the focus for Clare's work was therefore also with the parents' problems, accepting them for who they were and understanding their points of view, without judgement. By accepting the parent, it can also be a therapeutic experience for the child as well, to counteract their feelings of rejection. This may not be a novel idea today and certainly in social work. *The Munro Review* (Munro, 2011) focuses on listening to families and working in a compassionate way. However, during this historical period such narratives were not always part of the everyday culture for these families.

Clare Winnicott also acknowledged that for many children this was also an unfamiliar way of caring, with many orphanages and homes primarily focused on food and clothes rather than their emotional needs being met. Institutional child care therefore lacked something beyond happiness. Due to the war and the increased number of homeless children in Great Britain, many were entering institutional homes. Tension was growing about the concern regarding a lack of care and emotion in institutions. The favourable upbringing environment was therefore for a child to be in a stable family with the child becoming more accepted and welcomed (Kanter, 2018). The Curtis report published in 1946 also favoured adoption as the best option, with fostering being the next best thing. Institution care was deemed the least preferable option and wherever possible children retained contact with their relatives and siblings. In 1948 The Children Act meant local authorities were required to set up children's committees and appoint a children's officer to promote the welfare of deprived children. Institutional charities now had to take their place in a national system of child care and authority of the Home Office. The Children's Department also reduced the time children spent doing household chores and by 1965 substantial provision had been made by the local authorities (Higginbotham, 2017).

In the 1950s Clare Winnicott assisted children in Oxfordshire and the children included those with additional needs and emotional problems.

The children were placed in foster care and homes for the poor. In some of these situations Claire was asked by her superiors to support settings and address problems they had with the children in their care (Kanter, 2018).

In one situation Claire was asked to consult with the nursery that had suffered from an epidemic of bed wetting. She was anxious about her lack of expertise with such problems, but she went and listened carefully to the staff's account. She noted the highly structured daily routine and gently commented that the children did not get much time to themselves. The head reflected on this and realised that the children in the institution were restricted to remaining in their chairs all day and were frowned upon when they got messy. Clare supported the staff to discover that they needed to relax the institution structure (Kanter, 2018). From this visit the children moved around more, with freedom, and it is suggested relationships improved. The deputy medical officer also reported that the problem of bed wetting had cleared up shortly after Clare's visit (Kanter, 2018).

Clare Winnicott was one of a few psychiatric social workers who had become a psychoanalysist whilst still retaining her profession as social worker. By including her analytical training, she had a richer understanding about children from all walks of life (Kanter, 2018). This included the value of TO and, in Claire's case, notes from 1946 to 1947 described a two-year-old's use of a toy duck in making the transition from a foster place to an adoptive home. For Clare it was about understanding why a child clings to the past and how having an object brought with them aids the acceptance of the new environment. During that time many refugee children's belongings were taken away and burned. However, objects such as a favourite but filthy teddy bear were significant in having a connection from the past to the present for these children (Kanter, 2018). Garber's (2019) study also highlighted that, in high conflict divorce, the therapeutic creation and empowerment of TO to assist children experiencing separation anxiety, as well as the court's responsibility to encourage litigating parents to respect the child's needs for TO, still remains underestimated and an understudied area of the value and importance of emotional relationships.

In 1951 Donald Winnicott presented a paper on TO and transitional phenomena. But it was Clare's teaching that refers to TO as the first treasured possession. Clare Winnicott also discussed many of the core ideas that Donald, her husband, articulated more fully (Winnicott, 1951, 1956). The thinking is that, when the child care professionals enter the lives of these children, they must gain a holistic understanding about them as well as seeking to understand their internal feelings. This could be hidden in a memory, a fantasy, or a habit but by being able to make a link with their behaviour the child can then be better supported (Kanter, 2000).

The Winnicotts highlighted they were unconsciously trying to deal with observable behaviour in children, such as depression or grief at a loss, and therefore recovery was deemed possible. For them the most challenging children were those showing few signs that revealed their external circumstances and responses to their situation.

Clare's work with evacuated children in Oxfordshire was followed up by Winnicott's work in 1971, *Playing and Reality*. The influence of Donald Winnicott's work was particularly significant in social work residential care for children. He maintained a commitment to bringing a psychoanalytical perspective to the wider public, evident in his work with evacuated children during the war years in Oxfordshire, and, incidentally, where he met Clare, as well as his presence in state provision for children and families that had developed with the post-war growth of the welfare state (Horne and Lanyado, 2012, 2013).

Clare Winnicott (1954, cited in Kanter, 2018) emphasised the importance of the holding environment, defining it as a reliable environment in time and place, where the adults are able to hold the emotionally difficult situation with and for the child, so the child can tolerate it. This holding environment was maintained until the child was able to find a way through it as part of the natural healing process. The term 'holding' can also be useful to include the function of the family unit in a more sophisticated way, as well as the professional holding the child through clinical and, in the current context I include, formal day care (Kanter, 2018).

In the beginning the physical holding provides a psychology that can be good or bad. Good holding and handling facilitate the maturational process. However, what is deemed as bad holding means repeatedly interrupting those processes. The baby is a human being, immature and highly dependent and this has immense practical importance for acquiring experiences. During the early months the parent often intuitively knows, without any intellectual appreciation of what is happening, that the basis of feeding is not actually the feeding itself, but the beginning of object relating towards them. The relationship towards this new individual in their environment is therefore based on the way things begin and the patterns that gradually develop according to the relational experiences between baby and parent (Winnicott, 1953, 1992: p. 62).

Donald Winnicott and His Historical Relationships

During the mid-20th century two psychoanalysts, Anna Freud and Melanie Klein, represented extremes in the debate over the development of personality in childhood and how psychoanalysis can help to understand that development and treat psychological disorders. Anna Freud adhered strictly to her father Sigmund Freud's theory, believing that young children lacked the psychological development necessary for participating fully in adult forms of psychoanalysis treatment. Klein, on the other hand, considered children quite advanced at birth, with the death-instinct and its aggressive impulses being important. In contrast to these extremes, an independent school of object relations theorists developed with more moderate views. Donald Winnicott was one of the most influential of these more moderate theorists, as were Margaret Mahler and Heinz Kohut, regarding the 'Self Object'. Further considerations about how children were conceived by these pioneers will be discussed in the subsequent chapter and the focus will be on Winnicott's response to them in his own developing ideas of children (Caldwell, 2007).

Although already introduced, Donald Winnicott's (1896–1971) journey to psychoanalysis is an interesting one, which guides us to an appreciation of other eminent pioneers and psychoanalysts in the field during the same period. He was a paediatrician before becoming an analyst, so he already had clinical skills and brought a wealth of experience about observing children and mother–infant interactions to psychoanalysis. Already well respected for his medical treatment of children, Winnicott became increasingly interested in their emotional disorders. He joined a group of psychoanalysts being formed in London, under the guidance of Sigmund Freud (Winnicott et al., 1969). Winnicott continued his analysis with Joan Riviere, one of Klein's closest colleagues, and he was eventually supervised by Klein herself (Mitchell and Black, 1995), although he developed his own theories separately from those of Klein.

Winnicott observed the playful interaction between child and mother, in much the same way as Klein used her play technique. He liked to use the Squiggle Game, a technique that makes use of drawings by the child and the analyst, including the opportunity for each to make changes in the other's drawings. He believed that this process provided a special opportunity to create a contact with the child, in which it felt to him as if the child were alongside him helping to describe the case (Winnicott, 1971). Winnicott also felt it was important to focus on psychological health, and he defined this as something much more than simply making it through each day, going to work, and raising a family. For him he evaluated that a healthy individual lived three different lives:

1   A life in the world, with interpersonal relationships being key.
2   A personal psychic reality, including creativity and dreams.
3   Their cultural experience, although admitted that it was difficult to incorporate the cultural experience into the life of an individual.

However, he favoured the transitional space between the child and their parent and felt that it was dependent on the support offered to the child through their development (Winnicott, 1971). In considering the overall purpose of life, in contrast to Freud's perspective, Winnicott wrote:

> I have claimed that when we witness an infant's employment of a transitional object, the first non-me possession, we are witnessing both the child's first use of a symbol and the first experience of play.
>
> (p. 130)

The place where cultural experience is located is in the potential space between the individual and the environment (originally the object). The same can be said of playing. Cultural experience begins with creative living first manifested in play.

(p. 135)

The potential space is at the interplay between there being nothing but me and there being objects and phenomena outside omnipotent control.

(p. 135)

The Baby: Winnicott's Thinking about the Baby Thinking ...

Winnicott viewed the early years of life as being a time when the child must transition from a state of subjective supremacy toward one of objective reality. When a new-born is hungry, the breast appears. When a new-born is cold, it is wrapped in a blanket and warmed. The baby believes that it has created these conditions through its own needing, and so it feels supreme, or as Winnicott termed it, omnipotent (Winnicott, 1992). The mother's responsibility during this time would be to meet to the baby's every wish, as well as anticipate the needs of their baby. Subsequently, the baby does indeed have all their desired 'me', almost immediately. This subjective sense of self, as an empowered individual, is crucial to the core of personality as the child grows and represents the true self (Kernberg, 2018; Mitchell and Black, 1995; Winnicott, 1971).

For this development to progress in a healthy manner, the baby must have what Winnicott called a good enough mother (Winnicott, 1968b/2002). The good enough mother initially fulfils the baby's wishes immediately and completely, but then begins to withdraw when they are not needed. This creates an environment in which the baby is protected without realising it is being protected.

Over time, the mother slowly withdraws more from the immediate satisfaction of their baby's needs. This allows them to develop a sense of objective reality, the reality that the world does not immediately and completely satisfy anyone's desires and needs, and that wishing does not lead to satisfaction.

Questions to Consider

• What are your thoughts about the baby and their needs being met?
• What are your thoughts about a good enough mother?

Therefore, the good enough mother is not a perfect mother in the sense that she provides forever anything that the baby wants. Winnicott considered the unique condition of the good enough mother as appealing. A good enough mother starts off with a high degree of adaptation to the baby's needs. That is what 'good enough' means, this tremendous capacity for mothers to give themselves over to identification with the baby. The mother is laying down the basis for the mental health of the baby, as well as the dangers and conflicts that these bring to growth and development (Winnicott, 1968b/2002: 234). Although the mother is referred to, he did acknowledge that, during the baby's development, the father plays an important role too (Winnicott, 1968b/2002). Thus, in considering the overall development of the child, he acknowledges the role of good enough parents.

Question to Consider

- Donald Winnicott believed that healthy development required a child to have a good enough mother. Do you think you had a good enough mother (or father), and do you agree with this approach to raising an infant?

Good enough parents can be used by babies and young children, and 'good enough' means you and me. To be consistent, and so to be predictable for our children, we must be ourselves. If we are ourselves our children can get to know us. Certainly, if we are acting a part we shall be found out when we get caught without our make-up (Winnicott, 1968b/2002: 179).

Voice Vignette

For Winnicott, having loved ones available and tuned in will help to satisfy needs and desires to the best of the baby's ability. An individual living entirely in the realm of objective reality lacks the subjective core of their true self and cannot connect with others. Instead, they live in expectation of what others will do, influenced entirely by external stimuli (Mitchell and Black, 1995). Such babies, as individuals, develop what is called a false self-disorder (Winnicott, 1971). Although Winnicott described the false self as a successful defence, within the context of ongoing development, he did not consider it to be a condition of psychological good health (Winnicott, 1992).

Transitional Phenomena

Winnicott was the first child clinician and theoretician to have grasped the importance of the transitional phenomena, beginning with transitional space. From observing babies, he notes they used their hands and their fingers both to satisfy oral drives and to find peace (see Figure 2.1 with the thumb sucking). This is followed a few months later by activities of a different kind. The babies then benefit from an object such as a teddy bear, part of a cloth or a blanket to which they become attached in a habitual and authoritarian way. This is the Transitional Object. For Winnicott, the transitional experience is not just a concept, however, since it often involves TO. They do not exist merely as a substitute for the mother, they are also an extension of the child's own self. This allows the child to experience a world that is neither entirely within its control nor entirely beyond its control (Kernberg, 2004; Mitchell and Black, 1995). For Winnicott (1971), the journey from metaphorically merging with the mother toward a separate self from and related to its environment involves an 'intermediate' or 'transitional' space. This is a space for processing and interrelating the realities of the baby's inner and outer worlds. The relationship between the baby and their mother, as well as the relationships between the baby and their larger family, is actively involved in this transitional experience – the connection exists together, within a loving and supportive relationships (Winnicott, 1968b/2002).

It is within these relationships and spaces that the child must let go of their own illusions and appreciate they may have to wait for their needs to be satisfied. Unlike Freud (1905a), Winnicott views illusion as a positive aspect of development. That is, rather than being an obstruction to reality (delusional defences), illusion leads to the ability to play. Play allows for the emergence of culture, art, and religion. Because the task of reality acceptance is never completed for Winnicott, the movement from a distinctive inner reality toward an external one is a task humans continue to negotiate throughout their life. For Winnicott, this ability to play, to fantasise and create, is what allows new, original, sometimes surprising possibilities to emerge.

According to Winnicott, during the transition from the inability to distinguish oneself from one's objects to a state of clear differentiation, certain objects within the child's world become significant and are a bridge to the break between the infant's fantasy world where needs are unconditionally

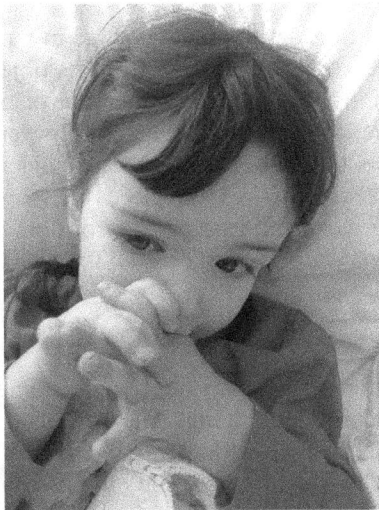

Figure 2.1 Transitioning from me to not me.

met, and the external world of reality where the meeting of needs is delayed. Transitional Objects therefore occupy a transitional space where reality is a combination of what the child brings to the object, as well as the object's external qualities. The objects have a reality for the child and should not be challenged. Rather, they should be given special status, recognising their value for the child (Parker, 2008).

Transitional objects assist the child in alleviating anxiety and enable their growing ability to recall an image of the mother's care during her absence. Transitional objects belong to an 'unchallenged' and 'intermediate' area contributed to by both the internal and external reality they serve (Winnicott, 1971, p. 2).

Question to Consider

Winnicott felt that TO were important for helping children to develop without too much anxiety. Did you have a favourite TO, and do you still have it? Do you think it is healthy for children to have such objects, and what might you do with your own children if you have them? If you already have children, do they have TO, and did you ever consciously expect them to have a TO?

Objects in an Infant's Life

Winnicott's insight into psychological reflections is his concept of object usage. The concept was his last major theoretical contribution and revisits and extends some of the ideas associated with his theory on transitional phenomena. In understanding Winnicott's concept he distinguishes object *usage* from object *relating*.

The latter term refers to a developmental stage in which the infant or child does not fully experience itself as separate from its objects. In object relating, the object to which one relates is more projection of one's internal fantasies and desires toward the object than an externally verifiable reality. Object usage, by contrast, refers to a later developmental achievement that recognises one's objects as objects with desires and needs of their own. Understanding and relating to the external world as separate from oneself with its own needs and desires is a complex journey (Parker, 2008).

Precursor Objects

The notion of a time interval between the two phenomena is important, with the TO presented as something quite different from oral excitement and satisfaction. It is the relationship with a concrete object that is no longer part of the child's body. It is the first 'not me' possession. The child therefore becomes passionately attached to their object and often only sleeps and is comforted when the object is nearby. This is usually observed by the object being brought to the mouth as the child strokes with their cheeks. They may even indulge in such auto erotic activities as thumb sucking, sometimes babbling, or by someone else humming as they play with the TO. In *Three Essays on the Theory of Sexuality*, with psychoanalysis, Sigmund Freud (1905b: 56) described the act of thumb sucking as the 'rhythmic repetition of a sucking contact by the mouth (or lips), pleasure sucking'.

Holding an object, stroking the face and sucking the thumb as they settle to sleep – Winnicott used the term transitional to describe the intermediate or third area between the thumb and the glasses (as in Figure 2.2), between the oral eroticism and the true object relationship, between primary creative activity and the projection of what has already been introduced, between primary awareness of indebtedness and the acknowledgement of indebtedness (Winnicott, 1951).

Winnicott termed such activities transitional phenomena. These phenomena are the defence against anxiety, against anxiety of the depressive type. The appearance of the TO is preceded, using precursor objects described by Gaddini and Gaddini (1970) and thus named by them, with Winnicott's agreement (1968). The TO is paradoxically created by the child, whereas the precursor objects, whilst still having the capacity to console the child in a unique way, are not discovered or invented by the child themselves (Gaddini and Gaddini, 1970). They are administered by the mother or parts of the child's own body, such as the thumb or part of the mother's body.

The element that precursor objects have in common is that have been introduced into the infant's mouth to integrate the self. The moment they get separated from the primary object such as the breast, the search for

Figure 2.2 Sucking thumb and stroking face.

integration is always with the oral stimulation, the mouth. The precursor object is therefore associated by the child in their search for tactile sensations such as the mother's hair, or even their ear.

The infant who sucks their thumb or has a pacifier does not reach out from himself and, although the precursor object is no longer the breast, it is also not separated from the child's own self. This suggests a continued dependence on the precursor object.

Transitional Objects

> I have claimed that when we witness an infant's employment of a transitional object, the first not-me possession, we are witnessing both the child's first use of a symbol and the first experience of play … The use of an object symbol symbolises the union of two now separate things, baby and mother, at the point in time and space of the initiation of their state of separateness.
>
> (Winnicott, 1971: 130)

During infant development, as a professional, caring for infants in group care such as formal day care settings, there is a tendency to use objects like Harlow's monkeys. For some babies their thumb is sucked, and they caress their hair with their fingers or use their fingers to stroke the upper lip. They may seek an external object such as a soft sheet or blanket to stroke and suck as they continue to suck their thumb or caress their own cheek. These items are significant when infants settle themselves to sleep or as a defence against anxious-inducing situations. Within this transitional phenomenon of experience, beginning to show between 4 and 12 months, the items then become known as Transitional Objects. Parents appreciate their value, and the smell and grubbiness of the cloth is part of the appeal, and parents may refrain from washing it, knowing this could destroy the value and meaning of the object to the infant (Winnicott, 1992).

Examples of Transitional Objects and Objects of Attachment: The Bunny

Cuddle cloths are open ended and can be whatever the child want them to be. A cuddle cloth can be named but can also be simply known as 'clothy'. It is often the smell and the fabric that is significant and for very young children this provides a sense of connection to their parents.

Winnicott (1951) focused on the special qualities observed in the relationship of the infant to the TO.

The core aspects of the TO are:

1   The infant assumes the rights over the objects.
2   The object is affectionately cuddled as well as excitedly loved and mutilated.
3   It must never change, unless changed by the infant.

4   It must service instinctual loving and also hating.

5   It must be seen by the infant to give warmth, or to move, or to have texture, or to do something that seems to show it has vitality or reality of its own.

6   It comes from without ... neither does it come from within.

7   The transitional object ... is not forgotten and it is not mourned. It loses meaning, and this is because the transitional phenomena have become diffused, have become spread out over the whole intermediate territory between inner psychic reality and the external world (Winnicott, 1971: 5).

Voice Vignettes: Examples of Transitional Objects

- Robert loved Ted and we went to a fair and we bought him a green stripe jumper. There was a book called *Little Bear Green Trousers*. Robert practised dressing and writing his name in the book. When he grew up, he gave the teddy to his nephew.
- Sam Lee had a soft blue elephant and his mum bought three more, identical elephants so that if one got lost there was always another.
- Amy had a long soft crocodile she used this to go to sleep on at nursery. She would lie down on top of it and sleep.
- Ivy had a Bunny, and it was named Ellie Bunny and was her favourite.
- Sam had a pink blanket with a silky hem all the way round it. She used it to rub it between her fingers and her index finger.

Winnicott's Key Themes about Transitional Objects

Some of the previous theories have been complex and perhaps challenging to those unfamiliar with some of the terms. In summarising some of the key areas, I have created some thoughts to consider.

Context Considerations

Consider the following and connect to how this would be helpful knowledge when working with infants and young children in formal day care:

- Winnicott (1951) therefore believed the connection to the TO was in bridging the inner world of the infant to the outer world. He saw the TO as initiating a sense of imaginative play and infants gaining a sense of their separateness to the environment they are in and a relationship to the outside world. He also considered the use of them positively and negatively and did not propose mothers initiate their use and extend the duration of TO in the popular assumption they are desirable and necessary for sound emotional development. For him, it was the spontaneity attachment of use and the inner creativity of the infant in processing their inner and outer reality.

- Transitional objects have been considered valuable for those infants settling into new environments and connecting the senses of the family home to a new external environment. The emphasis therefore would be directed towards reducing anxiety and the permanence of the object during times when external things and familiar people (parents) are 'hiding' or 'gone'. Winnicott makes a clear rationale for reflecting on the individual infant and allowing them to take the lead in what sooths them through this process rather than forcing an object upon them (Davis and Wallbridge, 2018).

- Transitional phenomena are thought to generally appear between the fourth and twelfth months depending on the baby. The object continues to be indispensable at certain moments of solitude, when falling asleep or when the child is threatened by a sense of depression. Many children gift a TO, and the name can be significant because it is usually a word that has come from the adults.

- Winnicott sums up the qualities of the relationship with the TO as the infant assuming rights over the object. The object is affectionately cuddled as well as excitedly loved and mutilated. It never changes unless changed by the infant, surviving instinctual loving and hating. The TO provides an outlet for aggression, as well as warmth and comfort. The symbolism of the TO distinguishes between fantasy and fact, between inner objects and external objects, between primary creativity and perception.

Examples of Transitional Objects and Objects of Attachment: The Teddy Drawing

Sometimes the teddy is not significant but what the teddy is wearing. A child I knew had a teddy who wore a shirt. It was a design the child had made on card, which had then been printed on the shirt. The activity was carried out by both the parent and the child, and the child needed it when the father had to travel away.

Voice Vignette

A child care worker described a three-year-old boy who walked around with a teddy bear tucked down his shirt like a baby kangaroo. When the care worker was taking the boy to an activity, he addressed the teddy bear and asked if he would like to come, too. 'Bear Bear's not real, you know', the child said earnestly.

- The importance to the child and the nature of the child's relationship with the object is probably the critical factor in saying whether it qualifies as a TO.

A Final Note

This chapter has aimed to introduce Clare and Donald Winnicott and who they were and how their thinking about TO evolved from not just a theoretical base but also a practical one working with children. I thought it was also important to consider what went before the TO and the development about how children self soothe and comfort through using a separate object. I have also included when this occurs and, in creating some thinking, provided a few examples for practice reflection.

References

Bowlby, J. (1969/1982) *Attachment and Loss: Vol. 1: Attachment.* New York: Basic Books.

Caldwell, L. (2007) *Winnicott and the Psychoanalytic Tradition.* London: Routledge.

Candlin, F. and Guins, R. (2009) *The Object Reader.* London: Routledge.

Davis, M. and Wallbridge, D. (2018) *Boundary and Space: An Introduction to the Work of D. W. Winnicott.* London: Routledge.

Fortuna, K., Baor, L., Israel, S., Abadi, A. and Knafo, A. (2014) Attachment to inanimate objects and early childcare: A twin study. *Frontiers in Psychology,* 5. https://doi.org/10.3389/fpsyg.2014.004

Freud, A. (1905a) *Normality and Pathology in Childhood Assessments of Development.* London: Karnac Books.

Freud, A. (1905b) *Three Essays on the Theory of Sexuality.* London: Karnac Books.

Gaddini, R. and Gaddini, E. (1970) Transitional objects and the process of individuation: A study in three different social groups. *Journal of the American Academy of Child Psychiatry,* 9 (2), 347–365. https://doi.org/10.1016/S0002-7138(09)61842-2

Garber, B. D. (2019) For the love of fluffy: Respecting, protecting, and empowering transitional objects in the context of high-conflict divorce. *Journal of Divorce & Remarriage,* 60 (7): 552–565. https://doi.org/10.1080/10502556.2019.1586370

Harlow, H. F. and Zimmermann, R. R. (1959) Affectional responses in the infant monkey. *Science,* 130, 421–432. https://doi.org/10.1126/science.130.3373.421

Harlow, H. F., Dodsworth, R. O. and Harlow, M. K. (1965) Total social isolation in monkeys. *Proceedings of the National Academy of Sciences,* 54 (1): 90–97. https://doi.org/10.1073/pnas.54.1.90

Higginbotham, P. (2017) *Children's Homes: A History of Institutional Care for Britain's Young.* Barnsley: Pen & Sword.

Horne, A. and Lanyado, M. (2012) *Winnicott's Children.* London: Routledge.

Horne, A. and Lanyado, M. (2013) *Independent Psychoanalytic Approaches with Children and Adolescents.* London: Routledge.

Kanter, J. (2000) The untold story of Clare and Donald Winnicott: How social work influenced modern psychoanalysis. *Clinical Social Work Journal,* 28 (3): 245–261. Available at: http://search.proquest.com/docview/227770208?accountid=1229

Kanter, J. (2018) *Face to Face Children: The Life and Work of Clare Winnicott.* London: Routledge.

Kernberg, O. F. (2004) Borderline personality disorder and borderline personality organization: Psychopathology and psychotherapy. In J. J. Magnavita (ed.),

Handbook of Personality Disorders: Theory and Practice. London: John Wiley & Sons, 92–119.

Litt, C. J. (1986) Theories of transitional object attachment: an overview. *International Journal of Behavioral Development*, 9: 383–399. https://doi.org/10.1177/016502548600900308

Mason, A. (2003) Melanie Klein, 1882–1960. *The American Journal of Psychiatry*, 160 (2): 241. Available at: http://search.proquest.com/docview/220484768?accountid=1229

Mitchell, S. A. and Black, M. J. (1995) *Freud and Beyond: A History of Modern Psychoanalytic Thought.* London: Basic Books.

Munro, E. (2011) *The Munro Review of Child Protection: Final Report – A Child-Centred System.* London: Department for Education. Available at: https://assets.publishing.service.gov.uk/government/uploads/system/uploads/attachment_data/file/175391/Munro-Review.pdf

Norman, A. (2019) *From Conception to Two.* London: Routledge.

Parker, S. (2008) Winnicott's object relations theory and the work of the holy spirit. *Journal of Psychology and Theology*, 36 (4): 285–293. Available at: https://journals.sagepub.com/doi/pdf/10.1177/009164710803600404?casa_token=FGnsXbjD0EcAAAAA:gWJOfy9m3ab8ruza6ljK15h_5vsfDs3NXvwQFvykADnPjP3OxURPUS2eeZqSFhlPmRwyZKhd6cM

Winnicott, D. W. (1951) *Transitional Objects and Transitional Phenomena.* London: Tavistock.

Winnicott, D. W. (1953) Transitional objects and transitional phenomena: A study of the first not-me possession. *International Journal of Psycho-Analysis*, 34: 89–97.

Winnicott, D. W. (1956) On transference. *International Journal of Psycho-analysis*, 37, 386–388.

Winnicott, D. W. (1968a) *Family and Individual Development.* London: Routledge.

Winnicott, D. W. (1968b/2002) *Winnicott.* The Squiggle Foundation. Available at: squiggle-foundation.org/winnicott/biography/

Winnicott, D. W., Winnicott, C., Shepherd, R., and Davis, M. (1969) *Development of the Theme of the Mother's Unconscious as Discovered in Psycho-Analytic Practice.* London: Routledge.

Winnicott, D. W. (1971) *Playing and Reality.* London: Tavistock.

Winnicott, D. W. (1992) *Babies and Their Mothers.* London: Merloyd Lawrence.

Chapter 3

Attachment, Object Relations, and Transitional Objects

Following on from the previous chapter, psychoanalysis and Winnicott's positionality will be extended, and this will move towards an examination about other key thinkers in this area, giving an introductory overview as well as a timeline in understanding key theories connected to child development and TO. Bowlby and attachment theory, creating a secure base, and separation anxiety will be included. Object Relations (OR) theory composed by Klein, Fairbairn, and Winnicott will also be discussed. OR refers not to the inanimate objects but the significant others who the child relates to. This is usually the primary carer as a whole person but can also be part of the person, such as the mother's breast. In developing a narrative about these concepts is the aim to emphasise the importance of nurturing young children. This should be within an encouraging and caring environment, with the child's needs met and their true self being able to emerge. This may lead on to Transitional Objects (TO) and these are introduced in relation to their value in the latter part of this chapter.

Why Theory?

The hospital doll: 48 years old and still a treasured doll with the history of being a TO as the child went to hospital (Figure 3.1). The doll was given to me by my Aunty. I remember feeling frightened as a four-year-old going to have my tonsils out in 1975 and taking two dolls for reassurance. I recall having to sleep in a cot which I felt was strange, being used to a bed. I remember the smell – coffee and chlorine. I remember crying and wanting to be home and jumping on the bed and being told off. The doll had my name on the back of its neck.

Often professionals are asked about why the children's toys in their care are so important and are they really that significant? Below are ten statements that I have accumulated when I have asked professionals regarding the justification about whether to leave the toys, engage with them, or remove them, especially as the child attends formal day care. I wonder at the end of the chapter whether each one could be challenged.

DOI: 10.4324/9781003296669-5

Figure 3.1 The hospital doll.

1 They often get lost so it's better they remain in drawers.
2 We spend ages looking for them and it's a nightmare, the blanket is too big and at three years old, as they enter preschool, we really try to discourage this and encourage them to leave them at home.
3 As they get older, I don't think they're transition objects, I think they're just items and stuff that keeps being brought in by the child and perhaps the family as well.
4 The parents are keener for the child to have a TO than the child.
5 Once the children come in and settle, we put the objects on the side so they can see them, but they can only have them at rest times.
6 Some children want to take or have other children's objects, so zero tolerance to having objects is an overall no to everyone.
7 They can interfere with their play, we encourage them and feel they are important in settling children.
8 I'm unsure if a dummy is a TO and if this is different to a cuddle cloth.
9 I think TO are valuable but after three years maybe not so much.
10 I think if they had a TO at school, it would be difficult for them.

Interestingly, not one respondent or students professionals and practitioners have been asked about or referred to the theory around TO. Elaborations on attachment and closeness were extended in conversations but very little was mentioned around the psychological understandings about infant child relationships and objects; this chapter aims to bridge that knowledge. Winnicott was a familiar name but the understanding of his theory was minimal in many of the interactions engaged with about the topic of TO.

Object Relational Perspective and the Developing Self

Object Relations Theory (OR) is a branch of psychodynamic thought that focuses on relationships being central to personality development (Greenberg, 1983). It highlights the importance of the identity-preceding structure, a personality structure formed out of interpersonal interactions. The view of the development of the self is bridged by Bowlby (1982), Mahler, Pine, and Bergman (1975), and Kohut (1971) in their work on relations. Kohut considered the relationship within, focusing on the three-part self. This, for him, can only develop when the needs of the individual self-states, including a sense of worth and well-being, are met in relationships with others.

In contrast to traditional psychoanalysis, which focuses on drives (instinctual motivations of sex and aggression), internal conflicts, and fantasies, self-psychology placed an increased emphasis on the variations of relationships. The self being formed in infancy and early childhood is from the internalising and processing interactions between the child and significant others. Although interactions are significant, the self is experienced subjectively, the sense of existence is both separate and as an interdependent being to that of others. The conditions necessary for the establishment of a self therefore include an initial period of an undifferentiated relationship, known as Winnicott's 'dual unity', with a mothering/caregiving figure, which then grows into a separate relationship. The child eventually recognises themselves as an individual, taking the form of a secure self. Concurrently, the carers of the child and the environment play a role in the security of the self by the presence of others. These are known as self-objects and continue to be important to self-maintenance and enhancement throughout life (Kohut, 1971; Mahler et al., 1975).

Object relations, dependency, and attachment, although interconnecting, are seen to differ substantially and, in exploring some of the key theorists, this develops thinking about attachment behaviour as well as the strength of attachment itself. Dependency and attachment are linked but each has a distinctive theoretical formulation of the origin and development of early interpersonal relations.

- Object relations is from the psychoanalytic instinct theory. The 'object' is usually conceived as being another person. It is generally agreed that the infant's first object is their mother. The origin of object relations, with the infant's initial relationship with his mother, is essentially oral in nature.
- Dependency was defined at first as a learned drive, acquired through its association with the reduction of primary drives.
- Psychoanalysts have historically used the term attachment when referring to specific love relations. Its current use in the psychological literature stems, however, from the familiar psychoanalyst, Bowlby (1958). While proposing a new approach to the child–carer relationship, a theory based on ethological principles, Bowlby sought a term to replace the term

'dependency' free of the theoretical connotations often attached to it. The term 'attachment' gained momentum with some ethologists and spread from them to psychologists studying animal behaviour. 'Attachment' refers to an affectional connection to one person. Attachment is thus discriminating and specific. Attachments occur at all ages and do not necessarily imply that attachment behaviour is associated with immaturity or helplessness (Ainsworth, 1969; Bowlby, 1953, 1969; Fairbairn, 1952).

In understanding the difference, further key pioneers throughout the 20th century are discussed. An inclusion of their own biography as well as their theoretical positions aims to create a better understanding about how they worked together, branched out alone, and differed in aspects of the theories proposed. It is intended as an introductory gallop with the aim to develop some reflective thinking and motivation for the reader to explore these thinkers further in-depth in their breadth of work. Many books and studies have focused on one key theorist in-depth as they developed thinking about infant relationships with humans and non-humans. This connection to them is therefore intended as a starting point for further interest areas and significance to those working with young children, beyond clinical practice.

Melanie Klein and Her Contribution to Infant Relationships

Melanie Klein was the fourth and last child to Jewish parents in Vienna; her elder sister died when Klein was four, and her elder brother died when she was 20. At the age of 21, after giving up training to be a doctor, she married her brother's friend, Arthur Klein. They had three children, but the marriage was unsettled and unhappy, with Klein becoming depressed. The Klein family moved around Central Europe for work, and it was in Budapest that Klein had a period of psychoanalytic treatment with Sándor Ferenzi, which sparked a lifelong interest in psychoanalysis and Freud's ideas (Klein, 1997).

Melanie Klein was deeply inspired by Sigmund Freud in the early 20th century, regarding her work with infants. Klein's clinical work, together with her direct observations of infants and their mothers, led her to a deeper understanding of the intricate internal facets at play during the first weeks and months of life. Klein focused on the way an infant may cope with extreme states of mind, from the intense pleasures and satisfaction of being held, fed, and loved, to the pains and frustrations of being left too long in a hungry or frightened state. Informed by Freud, Klein developed her own theories about infantile experiences, revealing the psychological lifelong impact of love and loss.

The Kleins then moved to Berlin in 1921 and Melanie Klein joined the Berlin Psychoanalytical Society. With the encouragement and interest of Karl Abraham, she began to analyse young children. In her work with children, Klein noticed that children's play and the toys they used carried important symbolic meaning for them, and that this could be analysed much in the same way as Freud analysed dreams with adults. This formed the basis of her subsequent clinical and theoretical thinking with major publications some years later, one titled, *The Psychoanalysis of Children* (1932/1997). Melanie Klein was considered controversial as well as a highly influential and powerful member of the British Psychoanalytical Society. Her theories about the development of a child's inner world transformed psychoanalysis and have had a deep and far-reaching impact that continues today. In consideration of Object Relations, Klein et al. (1952) described infants, as young as three weeks, interrupting their sucking to look at the mother's face, or, at two weeks older, responding to their mother's voice and smile with a change of facial expression. For her, this indicated 'gratification is as much related to the object which gives the food as to the food itself' (p. 239). Nevertheless, her theoretical account of the earliest period of development is much dominated by themes of food, orality, and the breast. The infant's first object relation is held to be to 'the loved and hated-good and bad-breast'. She believed that the infant has an inborn want, desire for the breast: 'the new-born infant unconsciously feels that an object of unique goodness exists, from which a maximal gratification could be obtained and that this object is the mother's breast' (p. 265). Although profoundly rooted in Sigmund Freud's thinking, Melanie Klein asserted that all human beings relate to others from birth (Klein, 1997, 1998).

Despite the obstacles Klein faced, as a female with no formal education and who suffered much personal tragedy, she pushed the boundaries of psychoanalysis. Her observations of the psychoanalytic encounter had original ideas about the formation of the internal world, and, most radical of all, she put the passions and experiences of the infant at the core of understanding about child development (Amos, 2010). Unlike the psychoanalytically informed approach to the education and socialisation of children that was used in the early 1920s in Vienna by Anna Freud, Klein's work was closely connected to adult psychoanalysis.

Klein would see the children at set times, like adult analysis, and she became more and more focused on their fears and anxieties as expressed in their play, and on the defences they used against them. This was an alternative and, in some sense, pioneering work with children, although it was less well received in Berlin, but more positively received in London.

Klein's son, Erich, and her daughter, Melitta, later a psychoanalyst in her own right, also joined her in London, but her eldest son, Hans, died in the Alps in 1934, aged 27. This was another personal tragedy and was considered to have influenced her work. As she grieved for her son, she continued to work, producing 'Mourning and Its Relation to Manic-Depressive States' (Klein, 1940). In these papers, Klein showed how the child becomes aware that they do not control their world but, instead, needs and depends on loving individuals in their presence. However, in the depressive position, the child feels they have attacked and destroyed aspects of these much-needed individuals, causing painful anguish. The characteristic of development in the depressive position is the capacity for concern and a wish to recompense for the damage the child feels they have done (Klein, 1997). During the Second World War she treated ten-year-old 'Richard'. The account of his analysis is written up as, 'The Narrative of a Child Analysis' (Klein, 1962) and this remains a vivid portrayal of her understanding of 'Richard's fears and anxieties at a turbulent moment in history.

Klein's Thinking about Loss and Mourning: The Depressive Position

Klein moved to London permanently, where she would spend the rest of her life working as a psychoanalyst and developing her highly original work. Undeterred by European criticism or opposition, Klein's curiosity in the inner world of her adult and child patients remained, and she continued developing her theoretical ideas with her clinical experience. Klein's work demonstrated that her psychoanalytic technique of understanding and interpreting anxieties, especially fear linked with aggressive impulses, could free up the patient and enable further exploration of their inner worlds.

Controversy and Development: The Paranoid–Schizoid Position

Klein saw the processes of projection and identification as two states, 'safety in sameness' in contrast to 'danger in difference'. If the source of what is desired and experienced as needed is not (objectively) present it is experienced instead as its opposite. This development includes a sense of having, oneself, contributed to the states of one's own wishing and feeling, longing, and loving as well as hating and feeling destructive.

Winnicott took an alternative position to Klein in understanding infants. Winnicott referred to the nurturing, emotional 'holding' of the child in their environment. Therefore, the best foundations for healthier development are presented by the provision of adults and the conditions necessary for adaptation and attunement. This ability in the primary carer (mother) and those others available to support her and her infant is crucial in promoting emotional development (Bott et al., 2011; Klein, 1997).

Klein's (1946) published work remains important, describing the primitive defence of 'splitting' in response to overwhelming anxiety, and delineates the 'paranoid–schizoid position', a universal mental state, from which the depressive position can emerge. Klein's understanding of primitive mental states enabled the treatment of psychotic patients and others who, until then, had not previously been thought suitable for analysis during this time.

In the 1940s and 1950s analysts grew around Klein, inspired by her work. They all went on to make their own very significant contributions to psychoanalysis. Wilfred Bion (1897–1979), Herbert Rosenfeld (1910–86), and Hanna Segal (1918–2011) were considered prominent figures following and taking her work forward.

Internal Objects (IO)

An Internal Object (IO) is defined as a mental and emotional image of an external object that has been taken inside the self. The character of the internal object is influenced by aspects of the self that have been projected into it. The most important internal objects are those derived from the parents, from the mother or breast onto which the infant projects its loving (life instinct) or hating (death instinct) aspects. These objects are internally experienced by the infant and causing pleasurable (good internal part–object breast) or painful (bad internal part–object breast). The infant's view of the motivation of these objects is based on both the perception of the external object as well as their desires and feelings that have been projected onto the external objects. Internal objects are experienced as relating to each other within the self and within Kleinian theory the state of the internal object is considered of prime importance to the development and mental health of the individual (Bott et al., 2011).

Questions to Consider

There are many more aspects of Klein's theory that have not been included and, as an intended introduction, areas such as the projected ego have not been fully included.

- What else could be read, researched, and understood about Klein that enhances how infant and child care is delivered today in the 21st century?
- How does this link to the mental health and well-being of young children in the 21st century?

Susan Sutherland Isaacs and Her Contribution to Childhood Development and Relationship with Klein

Susan Sutherland Isaacs was a writer and teacher. Growing up she was the second youngest of eight children, born Susan Fairhurst in 1885, near Bolton in Lancashire, to skilled working-class parents. Her father, William Fairhurst, was a saddler, and then a local journalist and lay Methodist preacher. Her mother, Miriam Sutherland, was a milliner, intellectual and musical. However, when Susan was six years old her mother died, and her father remarried. The family relationships were strained, and as an adolescent she religiously rebelled, identifying as a socialist. It was not until she was 23 years old that she was able to return to education. From Manchester she attended Newnham College Cambridge, where she undertook research into the psychology of children and spelling. By now a passion for child development in nursery and infant education was a special interest. After Teacher Training College, she married William Brierley in 1914, who was a botanist, moving with him to London. Their marriage ended in 1918 and at the age of 34, she became interested in psychoanalysis. She became an Associate Member at the British Psychoanalytical Society (BPAS) in 1921. She published her first book, *An Introduction to Psychology* (Isaacs, 1921), intended for non-specialists. Teaching a Workers' Educational Association class on psychology, she met Nathan Isaacs, whom she married the following year, and published her first psychoanalytically informed paper, as she began to develop psychoanalytic practice with adults and children. The following year, 1924, Geoffrey Pyke set up a progressive school for young children in Cambridge, the Malting House School, and Susan Isaacs was appointed as the first principal to lead it. The school was child-centred in its principles, with few constraints and plenty of opportunity for children to explore their environment. The teachers would answer questions, rather than instruct the children. Klein's views on the importance of sexual enlightenment on intellectual development were also influential, and Klein visited the school in its first year, while on a visit to Britain (Klein, 1927, 1929).

Unfortunately, the school had its challenges and, as a result, it closed. Isaacs returned to London where she worked on the detailed observations she had carried out at the school. This culminated in a book, *Intellectual Growth in Children* (Isaacs, 1930). She then grounded her work in the ideas about how children learn from their own observations and experiences, and was known to be part of Klein's circle (Graham, 2009). Isaacs built on Klein's clinical insights to construct a conceptual framework for the study of emotional and cognitive development. In a break with Freudian tradition, she claimed that phantasy was present from the beginning of life. In fact, emanating from earliest bodily experience, phantasies are seen as rudimentary thought processes, from which will spring object relations, language, and self-awareness (Isaacs, 1948; Graham, 2009).

Aspects of the argument she made include:

- The transference situation is almost entirely a construct of unconscious phantasy.
- External realities are progressively woven into the texture of phantasy, but the source of phantasy is internal, in the instinctual impulses.
- Phantasy is taken to represent the subject's psychic reality.
- Play is central for learning, and the innate curiosity of the child.

Using the name 'Ursula Wise', she also began an influential regular advice column in the magazine, *Nursery World*, which can today be found in the Froebel Archive in London. Her books were based on observations she'd made at the Malting House School, but always underpinned by psychoanalytic understanding. In 1933 Isaacs was appointed Director of the newly established Department of Child Development at the Institute of Education in London, and within six years she had built up an international reputation for the department (Isaacs, 1940, 1948).

Anna Freud and the (Dis)Connection with Klein

Anna Freud was born in 1895 in Vienna, the sixth and youngest child of Sigmund Freud and Martha Bernays. From early childhood, she admired her father greatly and by the age of fourteen was already interested in psychoanalysis. In 1917 she started work as a primary school teacher. During her protracted recovery from tuberculosis, she read the writings of her father and his colleagues, which galvanised her determination to become a psychoanalyst.

She started her own analysis with her father, not an unusual occurrence for the time. She continued to study the psychoanalytic literature and started work with patients. She became a Member of the Vienna Psychoanalytic Society in 1922 and began to work psychoanalytically with children. In 1925 she became Secretary of the International Psychoanalytical Association (IPA), and in 1927 she published 'Introduction to the Technique of Child Analysis' (King and Steiner, 1991).

According to Sigmund Freud, the human mind could be divided up into three distinct parts: the id, the ego, and the superego, and he outlines several ego defences. Anna's work upheld her father's theory, and she explored ego psychology and the ten defence mechanisms, highlighting that they could pose difficulties if used to prevent a person from coping with their underlying anxiety (Kelly, 2023). Anna Freud was most likely influenced by Melanie Klein (for example, by eliminating the introductory phase of the analysis for a child and realising the value of play as a means for understanding the child). However, they appear to diverge significantly in crucial ways. Melanie Klein, for example, thought that child psychoanalysis could be helpful for all children as an aid in the modulation of their anxieties, while Anna Freud felt that analysis was only appropriate when a child has developed infantile neurosis. Melanie Klein also thought that children's play was like free associations whilst Klein made interpretations related to, for example, the child's curiosity about their mother. Anna Freud did not believe that a child's play could be considered the same as an adult's free association. She felt that the analyst was required to build up an understanding of what the child is expressing over many play sessions, considering the child's verbalizations as well, before making an interpretation. She and Klein therefore had differing views about the theory and practice of child psychoanalysis.

In 1937 she opened the Jackson Nursery in Vienna for extremely deprived toddlers. This was closed in 1938 due to the arrival of the Nazis, and the Freuds subsequently fled Austria. Ernest Jones (former IPA President) devoted great energy and remarkable skill to bringing them safely to London and

Anna Freud remained deeply indebted to him (Freud, 1966). In 1941, Anna Freud, with her friend and colleague Dorothy Burlingham, opened 'The Hampstead War Nurseries', caring for infants, toddlers, and young children separated from their families. In-service training required staff to write detailed observations about the children's daily behaviour. These observations were discussed every evening with Anna Freud and Dorothy Burlingham and their understanding became crucial in helping to refine insight into the child's normal and pathological development. The Hampstead Child Therapy Course and Clinic was then established as a nonprofit to provide treatment, training, and observational research in child psychology.

Anna Freud demonstrated a deep dedication in sharing her analytic understanding with all those who encountered children, and was a strong voice alongside James and Joyce Robertson, John Bowlby, and Isabel Menzies Lyth in studying the impact of hospitalisation and separation on young children (Sandler, 2015). The Hampstead Child Therapy Course and Clinic was renamed the Anna Freud Centre for Children and Families in 1984 and remains open today, treating and educating within the field of mental health and well-being.

Fairbairn and His Contributions to Object Relations: An Introduction

William Fairbairn was born in Edinburgh 1889, the only child of Thomas and Cecilia Fairbairn. He studied Divinity and Hellenic Greek at Edinburgh University, and in Kiel, Strasbourg, and Manchester. His family were also religious, and he considered himself a Christian. Fairbairn always lived and worked in Edinburgh, leaving only when he served during the war. Fairbairn's experiences in the War had had a deep impact on him, and he would treat many ex-soldiers suffering from trauma, known as war neuroses. While studying to become a psychiatrist, Fairbairn read the work of Sigmund Freud and Carl Jung. Shortly after qualifying, Fairbairn began to practice psychoanalysis himself. Between 1928 and 1930 Fairbairn began to depart from Freud's account of several core analytic principles: the structure of the psyche, the theory of instincts, and repression. Fairbairn was not satisfied with Freud's structuring of the psyche, especially his description of the relationships between the ego, super-ego, and id (Fairbairn, 1956).

Today he is known as the 'father of object relations', and this was because of his important innovations and developments in that branch of psychoanalytic theory. In Fairbairn's theoretical work, relatedness and relationships remain at the centre of human psychology and experience. After the First World War, Fairbairn decided to move away from his theological and philosophical studies, and into psychiatry. He entered immediately into his medical training and qualified in 1924.

In the mid-1930s Fairbairn withdrew from his university position and went into psychoanalytic practice. Many believe that, by living in Edinburgh, a professional separateness from the Society based in London occurred and contributed to the originality of Fairbairn's concepts. Despite the perceived disconnection, his ideas were deeply informed by his colleagues in London, and his work, in turn, went on to have a profound influence on British object relations theory, becoming one of the key figures of the independent tradition (Gomez, 2017).

During the 1930s Fairbairn followed Melanie Klein's theories, particularly about child development. He was inspired by Klein's account of innate destructive urges and their attendant desire for reparation and restitution. In turn, Fairbairn began to influence Klein's thinking and that of her colleagues. His innovative, bold work in object relations paved the way for alternative theoretical and clinical approaches.

In Fairbairn's experience, analysing the Oedipus complex in his patients as Sigmund Freud had done did not always lead to a resolution of their problems, and this dissatisfaction led him to develop the theory of schizoid phenomena. This would also later inspire Klein to alter her 'paranoid position' to 'paranoid–schizoid position', and that would similarly have a considerable impact on Donald Winnicott's thinking about schizoid states. Fairbairn conceptualised the child as metaphorically splitting off the emotionally responsive side of his or her parents from the unresponsive side, thereby creating 'good' and 'bad' objects, and often also splitting the ego into 'good' and 'bad', a process often leading to borderline states. His development of a quite new theoretical and clinical approach to borderline states remains very important in the psychological treatment with patients (Clarke, 2018; Gomez, 2017).

Fairbairn also objected to the notion that the internalisation of external objects was based on the death instinct, as offered by Klein. The death instinct is a remnant of the Freudian model that was emphasised in Klein's model, and her model assumes that human behaviour is motivated by a struggle between the instinctual forces of love and hate. Whilst Fairbairn's model also emphasised the internalisation of external objects, his was not based on instinctual drives, but rather the child's normal desire to understand the world around him, which I think resonates to how practitioners support children's learning and development today. Fairbairn began his theory with his observation of the child's absolute dependency on the good will of its mother. The infant, Fairbairn noted, was dependent on its maternal object (or caretaker) for providing him with all his physical and psychological needs (1956).

One of Fairbairn's major theoretical developments was the search for relationships, and that this is more urgent than the desire to gratify instincts. For him the driving force in the human psyche is not the pleasure principle, but a fundamental need to relate to and connect with other objects, and other people. Fairbairn's emphasis on the centrality of relationships in the psyche was a great inspiration to John Bowlby and played a key role in the development of Bowlby's famous 'attachment theory' (Gomez, 1994).

Bowlby: Attachment and Care

Bowlby (1969) considered infants to have an innate and evolutionary need to be close to an adult carer, predominately the parent, seeking care and comfort. The way infants develop emotionally is determined predominately by the sensitivity and characteristics of their parents. The more sensitive and reliable, the more secure attachment flourishes. Tuning in to an infant's behaviour and feelings enables the infant to regulate their own emotions and begin to make sense of how they feel themselves. There is also recognition that attachment is not 'fixed' and Dozier et al.'s (2006) studies of adopted children evoke attention to 'attachment biobehavioural catch up' (ABC), educating the parents about the behaviour they observe in infants. They evaluated that the effects of disrupted attachments can be reduced and how negative experiences in early life do not necessary determine a life's emotional trajectory. Parents were taught to observe and read infants rejecting any ambivalent behaviour as an expected response to their nurturing and provision of positive care. Parents were supported in offering care and bonds when it is not physically sought by the children in a way of re-regulating their emotional and social capacities. By reflecting on practice, parents reviewed and moved forward through effective interactions during everyday care routines supporting the emotional well-being of young infants in their care.

Understanding Attachment: Past to Present

Richard Bowlby, John's son, during an interview about his father, evaluated that his father was not afraid to confront intimidating figures, which was to lead him into a series of conflicts throughout his career (Bowlby, 2019). This began with his psychoanalytical training when he would insist on arguing with his analyst Joan Riviera and his supervisor Melanie Klein. He found it hard to accept their rigidly held theories because he believed these did not satisfy the scientific rigour he had learned at Cambridge when studying medicine in 1949. He considered everything was too clinical (recall the way Klein met her clients/children). In 1949 the World Health Organization invited John Bowlby to report on the psychiatric needs of the many homeless children who had been orphaned because of the Second World War. The wide-ranging material that he gathered for the World Health Organization report was called 'Maternal Care and Mental Health' (Bowlby, 1951). He believed a warm, intimate, and continuous relationship with the infant's mother or permanent mother substitute, in which both find satisfying enjoyment, was necessary for healthy development of the infant to occur. However, a criticism was his use of the words 'permanent mother substitute' by adding one person who steadily 'mothers' him. Today we acknowledge that the word carer may be the father or someone who is primary in the care. Bowlby felt the same and this was noted in his later writings. Bowlby also made the mistake of referring to the word 'continuous' and this was problematic and misinterpreted. He did not distinguish between what he meant by a 'continuous, enduring' relationship. For him, though, he was talking about separation of potentially six months or more between the primary carer and child not the intermittent break in care throughout the day such as going to work and leaving the child for short periods. He was primarily addressing children's experience of complete maternal deprivation or prolonged separation when abandoned in orphanages. It was these more extreme situations that he considered contributed to delinquent character behaviour (Bowlby, 2019: 12). He agreed that in typical circumstances it is healthy for children to be left with relatives or carers for short periods, knowing they will return.

In contemporary society we continue to share a discourse about the value of attachment, considering the connections to neuroscience and understanding brain processes. However, attachment has also been argued to be a theory in supporting and maintaining maternal relationships, potentially excluding other relationships. I have not attempted to include a critique of attachment theory but rather map the historical theoretical and practice influences that culminated in the contemporary thinking about attachment within formal day care.

John Bowlby (1907–90) was the fourth child of six in an upper-middle-class family and, similar to most upper-middle-class families, children were often cared for by a 'nanny' and 'nurse maids'. Children would live in the nursery on the top floor of the house and the children were taken to the parents.

John was cared for by his nurse maid called 'Minnie' who left when he was four years old, and he describes the experience being like the loss of a mother. As an adult he trained as a doctor and then as a psychoanalyst (1936–39) working in Child Guidance with young offenders. For him, what distinguished these young offenders from others attending the Child Guidance Clinic was their family history. They predominantly came from broken families, with few continuing relationships. Bowlby published *Child Care and the Growth of Love* (1953) and in (1969) his trilogy *Attachment, Separation, and Loss*. These three books summarised human attachment behaviour.

Question to Consider

• Do you consider the historical period significant to attachment?

In taking a critical lens, observational behaviour evaluates the emotions of children, culminating in practitioners making assumptions about what their internal feelings are. Behaviourist perspective of attachment (Dollard and Miller, 1950) suggested that attachment is a set of learned behaviours. The basis for the learning of attachments was the provision of food and an infant will initially form an attachment to whoever feeds them. They learn to associate the feeder (usually the mother) with the comfort of being fed and, through the process of classical conditioning, come to find contact with the mother comforting. They also found certain behaviours such as crying and smiling convey desirable responses such as attention and comfort from others and, through the process of operant conditioning, learn to repeat these behaviours to get the things they want.

Schaffer and Emerson (1964) also identified how attachment could be framed into a sequential mode through their observations. They studied 60 infants at monthly intervals for the first 18 months of life. The children were all studied in their own home, and a regular pattern was identified in the development of attachment. There have since been studies to dispute the areas within this frame, such as a preference for the mother to that of another, from a very early age. However, Schaffer and Emerson continue to be drawn on in critically reflecting on the broad sequential progression of attachment proposed. Three measures were recorded in the study:

- Stranger Anxiety – response to the arrival of a stranger.
- Separation Anxiety – distress level when separated from a parent, the degree of comfort needed on return.
- Social Referencing – the degree a child looks at their carer to check how they should respond to something new (secure base).

They discovered that infant's attachments develop in the following sequence:

- Asocial (0 to 6 weeks)

  They considered young infants as being asocial in that many kinds of stimuli, both social and non-social, produce a favourable reaction, such as a smile. In a sense they have not discriminated but are beginning to learn about their environment.

- Indiscriminate Attachments (6 weeks to 7 months)

  Arguable, infants indiscriminately enjoy human company, and most infants respond equally to any caregiver. They get upset when an individual ceases to interact with them.

  From 3 months, infants smile more at familiar faces and can be easily comforted by a regular caregiver.

- Specific Attachment (7 to 9 months)

  Special preference for a single attachment figure. The infant looks to familiar carers for security, comfort, and protection. They show fear of strangers (stranger fear) and unhappiness when separated from a special person (separation anxiety).

- Multiple Attachment (10 months and onwards)

The infant becomes increasingly independent and forms several attachments. By 18 months many infants have formed multiple attachments.

The results of the study indicated that attachments were most likely to form with those who responded accurately to the infant's signals and not necessarily the person they spent more time with. Schaffer and Emerson (1964) called this sensitive responsiveness. Intensely attached infants had mothers who responded quickly to their demands and interacted with their child. Infants who were weakly attached had mothers who failed to interact. Many of the infants had several attachments by ten months old, including attachments to mothers, fathers, grandparents, siblings, and neighbours. For the majority, however, the mother was the main attachment figure for about half of the children at 18 months old and the father for most of the others. The ethological theory of attachment (e.g., Bowlby, Harlow, Lorenz) suggested that infants are biologically pre-programmed to form attachments with others, and the infant produces innate 'social releaser' behaviours such as crying and smiling that stimulate innate caregiving responses from adults.

In Harlow and Zimmerman's (1959) study of attachment with monkeys, he evaluated that it does not always have to be reciprocal, and an individual may have an initial attachment to another which is not shared. We now know emotional relationships are complex and require the active ongoing intersubjectivity and tuning in of both carer's and infant's attachment to be successful. Harlow's experiments on rearing monkeys took several forms and he concluded that infants reared without a 'real' mother figure were:

- More timid.
- They didn't know how to act with other monkeys.
- They were easily bullied and wouldn't stand up for themselves.
- They had difficulty with mating when they were older.
- The female monkeys became inadequate mothers when they reached adulthood (Harlow and Zimmerman, 1959).

Other physically observed behaviours included that, when the monkeys were exposed to prolonged stress, their stools were softer and they had digestive problems. These behaviours were observed only in the monkeys who were left with the surrogate mothers for more than 90 days. For those left for fewer than 90 days, the effects could be reversed if placed in a normal environment where they could form attachments. He concluded early positive parenting was vital in an infant's life for healthy development, although negative exposure could be reversed in monkeys if an attachment was made before the end of the critical period (Berk, 2015). This is positive and hopeful in supporting a fruitful outcome even when young infants have had adverse childhood experiences. These are that,

- Deficits that occur in the early years may be overcome with later enrichment, though the process will likely be more difficult.
- The brain has plasticity and can recover over time with positive support and consistent emotional relationships.

Rutter (2002) considered the importance of emotional development and maternal deprivation as a 'vulnerability factor' rather than a causative agent, with several varied influences determining which life path a child will take. In 1989, Rutter led the English and Romanian Adoptees Study Team, following many of the orphans who had been exposed to extreme neglect and deprivation in their earliest years through to their adoption into Western families. They were observed and studied during their latter childhood into their teens in a series of substantial studies, focusing on the effects of early privation and deprivation. The Study Team concluded that attachment and the development of new relationships were successful, yielding some reason for optimism that if an infant is removed from an emotionally deprived environment and placed in a positive and warm environment, emotional growth can occur.

Ainsworth (1913–99), working with Bowlby, drew on what she termed the 'Strange Situation' in understanding the importance of close relationships and emotional attachments. Ainsworth's (1979) Strange Situation used structured observational research to assess and measure the quality of attachment. It has eight predetermined stages, including the mother leaving the child for a short while, playing with available toys in the presence of a stranger, being alone, and the mother returning to the child.

Stage 1 – Mother and child enter the playroom.
Stage 2 – The child is encouraged to explore.
Stage 3 – Stranger enters and attempts to interact.
Stage 4 – Mothers leaves while the stranger is present.
Stage 5 – Mother enters and the stranger leaves.
Stage 6 – Mother leaves.
Stage 7 – Stranger returns.
Stage 8 – Mother returns and interacts with child.

The results highlight the role of the mother's/significant and consistent carer's behaviour in determining the quality of attachment (Cohen and Waite-Shipansky, 2017, cited in Ainsworth, 1979). This led to the conceptualisation of the Caregiver Sensitivity Hypothesis, which suggests that a mother's behaviour towards their infant predicts their attachment type (Ainsworth, 1979). Whilst there has been criticism of this experiment and the limitations to being able to connect with the internal feelings of the infant, it does provide some thinking about behaviours that perhaps we assume and interpret as something else. In reflecting on behaviours and scenarios we move closer to thinking about how we support those infants during transitional periods (Degotardi and Pearson, 2014). This will be an area further discussed in the subsequent chapters.

Typically, a child's response to the Strange Situation follows one of four patterns:

1   Securely attached children: free exploration and happiness displayed upon the mother's return. If he cries, he approaches his mother and holds her tightly and is comforted by being held. Once comforted, he is keen to resume his independent exploration.
2   Avoidant-insecure children: little exploration, and little emotional response to the mother. Little emotion observed when her mother leaves and tends to avoid or ignore her when she returns (Ainsworth, 1979).
3   Resistant-insecure (also called 'anxious' or 'ambivalent') children: little exploration is carried out in the room and there is greater separation anxiety. There is an ambivalent response to the mother upon her return (Ainsworth, 1979).
4   Disorganised-insecure children: little exploration, and a confused response to the mother. The disorganised child may exhibit a mix of avoidant and resistant behaviours. The main theme here is one of confusion and anxiety (Main and Solomon, 1986).

Question to Consider

• What does this mean in practice?

Caregiving routines make up a large part of a child's day and provide practitioners with many opportunities to involve them in caregiving experiences through respectful, reciprocal, and responsive interactions. The daily routine should include time for interactions to be nurtured, introduced, established, and maintained – an opportunity for the infant's development. Learning and well-being should be conveyed in a way that responds to the infant's individuality, deepening their relationship with their carer (Tankersley, Vonta, and Ionescu, 2015).

Respectful care is about inclusivity and creating opportunities for trusting relationships together. During mealtimes, for example, a childs teddy is read a story with the children and together they share moments of connectivity, whilst enabling child autonomy in feeding themselves.

Respectful caring is the key to growing trusting relationships and intellectually stimulating education; we find ourselves doing it 'with' children instead of doing it 'to' children (Pikler, 1972). Bowlby's interest in the external relationship was at odds with the psychoanalysts of the time, and they purported that he did not place enough emphasis on the inner world (Ainsworth, 1969).

Object Relations Theory Today: An Overview and the Theoretical Positions

There are those who say that it is inappropriate to refer to object relations theory as if it were a single theory. It is more appropriate to refer to object relations regarding a group of psychoanalysts and theorists who share a common interest in object relations, but whose theories tend to vary with each individual theorist. Sigmund Freud used the term 'object' to refer to any target of instinctual impulses. In the current context, an object is a person, or some substitute for a person, such as a blanket or a teddy bear, which is the aim of the relational needs of a developing child. Melanie Klein is generally recognized as the first object relations theorist, and her change in emphasis from Sigmund Freud's view was rather profound. Freud believed that a child is born more like an animal than a human, driven entirely by instinctual impulses. Only after the ego and the superego begin to develop is the child psychologically human. Klein, however, felt that an infant is born with drives that include human objects and the corresponding need for relationships. In other words, the infant's instinctual impulses are designed to help the child adapt to the distinctly human world into which the child is born (Mitchell and Black, 1995). The focus of object relations theory is to understand a person's current relationships in terms of how their childhood attachments to objects affected their development.

There have been many theories over the years about how the human psyche is formed. Some believe all knowledge is presented within the realm of existence, but others feel humans are born with unconscious processes already at play. Object relations theory suggests that a person's behaviour was created through their interpersonal relationships. While both Freud and Klein believed relationships with others play a part in behaviour, Klein didn't subscribe to the sexual pleasure aspect of Freud's work. She felt the need to form relationships and human contact were the keys to understanding behaviour.

- The self perceives the object.
- The person perceives themselves in relation to that object.
- The person perceives the relationship/connection between themselves and the object.

It's important to understand that the term 'object' in object relations does not mean an actual inanimate object as Winnicott's 'transitional object'. The object references can be a person or experience connected to an individual. The term 'object' acts as an overarching label for an external connection. How a person perceives their relationships to be with others and how they perceive themselves in return are two main parts of the connection. For example, the object in question could be a mother's consistent or inconsistent care, which Klein believed would directly correlate with the child's personality. The more a mother cares for the child with consistent acts, such as breastfeeding, playtime, and loving support, would deeply affect how the child perceives the mother, themself, and their connection. In turn, this would lead to a positive or negative ability to form relationships as an adult.

Winnicott: Bridging Object Relations to Winnicott Theory

According to Winnicott (1966, 1987), infants are born into an interpersonal context that includes certain expectations regarding the child. Winnicott notes that during the last few months of pregnancy and for the first few weeks after the infant's birth, the mother becomes preoccupied with her infant, a state that he called 'primary maternal preoccupation'. It is a state involving fantasies of and about the infant that makes the mother especially attuned to her infant's needs. This temporary hyper-attentiveness to the infant's needs creates an environment in which the infant experiences itself as 'omnipotent' and the 'creator' of its environment. Winnicott sees the mother's attunement to the infant's needs for feeding as creating a 'moment of illusion' in which the infant's wishes for and envisioning of a solution for its needs co-occurs with the mother's presentation of her breast. This co-occurrence gives the infant the subjective experience that it created the breast that appeared and that it therefore controls its environment.

These experiences become the basis for a later sense of a creative, capable self for Winnicott. Without this temporary, but necessary, experience of subjective authority, the child's belief in its own creativity and power is undermined and the emergence of the true self is hindered. Both in the mother's expectations for the infant and in her connection to her infant in a well-timed, synchronistic manner, the mother provides a 'holding environment' that allows the infant to begin to piece together self and others. During interactions with her infant, the mother functions similarly to a mirror, whereby the infant can perceive a reflection of their own experience and gestures. Winnicott's chief metaphor for this ability to perceive oneself through the (m)other is the eye contact between mother and infant. Through these reciprocal exchanges, the infant has a sense of growing future experiences of self and others. Therefore, the mother's task is twofold for Winnicott (1966, 1971b). First, she must temporarily provide and allow for the infant's illusion of omnipotence through her early hyper-attentiveness. However, once this sense of illusion is established, she must then 'disillusion' the child. The mother's initial 'perfect' adaptability to the child's needs must give way to a 'good enough mothering' in which she returns to an awareness of and tending to her own needs and constraints. There are two concepts to Winnicott's way of envisioning the movement from the state of merger to the recognition of self and environment as separate. These are his concepts of transitional phenomena and that of object usage. Regarded as an umbrella term, transitional phenomena refers to a cluster of related concepts including Winnicott's proposals regarding 'transitional objects', 'potential space', 'illusion', and use of symbols. Object usage refers to a developmental achievement in which the child can recognise the objectivity of its environment and interact with others in ways that recognise the other as a person in his or her own right (Parker, 2008).

Winnicott reaffirms his belief in the crucial importance of the environment, and the value of the objects within it. This chapter ends with how Winnicott bridges the previous theories, from the internal, external reality of objects, separate from care and separate from the children themselves.

Voice Vignette: The Physical and Emotional Loss of a TO

'My Boo-Boo provided me with the comfort and security I craved. I wanted it with me, a bit like I wanted my mum with me all the time when I was little', he says.

The owner of Boo-Boo continues to reveal that shortly before his first day at school, his mother told him that he could not take his Boo-Boo with him and that he should throw it into their fire. 'I can see it now, the lounge and the open fire, my mum telling me that I had to throw this Boo-Boo in. I couldn't have it anymore, I had to grow up. I can't remember whether I cried or not, I can just feel the anguish. I had a sense of loss, an emptiness, without understanding.'

The owner does not resent his mother, now 90 years of age, about what happened: 'It was a rite of passage; I detected that it was for my own benefit. It doesn't cause me distress, I never felt traumatised, it's not anything I ever dwelt on', he says. But he acknowledges that the clarity of the scene as it replays in his mind, the fondness with which he remembers his Boo-Boo and the meaning we now know these objects can have for children all suggest this may not be the whole story (Sarner, 2018, n.p.).

Similarly, Linus, the best friend of Charlie Brown and the younger brother of Lucy van Pelt in the comic strip *Peanuts*, highlighted the impact of the TO. The cartoonist Charles M. Schulz popularised the term 'security blanket' and Linus was rarely seen without his. The cartoonist's widow, Jean, reported that the idea came from her husband's youngest child, Jill, who used to carry a blanket everywhere. 'In fact, she would get out of her bed and sleep curled up on the floor with her blanket outside of the parents' room', she says. 'So, that's kind of sweet-talk about security' (Sarner 2018; Schwartz, 2012).

Appreciating the subjectivity of oneself in other people's lives is a fundamental indicator of social development. Winnicott was also interested in how it is possible to be with another person without necessarily being observably, actively engaged with that person. He called this 'the capacity to be alone'. There is a paradox in this in that 'this experience is that of being alone, as an infant and small child, in the presence of mother'. Therefore, the basis of the capacity to be alone is a paradox; it is the experience of being alone while someone is present. The essential ingredient is the capacity to act without the need to involve the other person in doing something or to provoke an experience in the other – making her feel she has been 'done-to' – to carry on with the activity. It is a state in which the processes of projective identification are not called upon (Winnicott, 1971a: 149).

A Final Note

Reflect again on the ten questions introduced at the beginning of the chapter. How would they be responded to now?

1 They often get lost so it's better they remain in drawers.
2 We spend ages looking for them and it's a nightmare, the blanket is too big and at three years old as they enter preschool, we really try to discourage this and encourage them to leave them at home.
3 As they get older, I don't think they're transition objects, I think they're just items and stuff that keeps being brought in by the child and perhaps the family as well.
4 The parents are keener for the child to have a TO than the child.
5 Once the children come in and settle, we put the objects on the side so they can see them, but they can only have them at rest times.
6 Some children want other children's objects, so we have a zero tolerance and tend to say no to everyone who wants to bring in an object.
7 They can interfere with their play, we encourage them and feel they are important in settling children.
8 I'm unsure if a dummy is a TO and if this is different to a cuddle cloth.
9 I think TO are valuable but after three years maybe not so much.
10 I think if they had a TO at school, it would be difficult for them.

Whilst much of this chapter has been descriptive in sharing the biographies of key theories, it hopes to create space to be able to connect the chronological journeys taken by each one and where their interests rested and with whom they related. In omitting some but including others, I made the decision about who I think would be helpful in working with children in formal day care settings, connecting early education with psychoanalysis.

References

Ainsworth, M. (1969) Object relations, dependency, and attachment: a theoretical review of the infant-mother relationship. *Child Development*, 40: 969–1025. Available at: www.psychology.sunysb.edu/attachment/courses/620/pdf_files/attach_depend.pdf
Ainsworth, M. (1979) Infant–mother attachment. *American Psychologist*, 34 (10): 932–937. http://dx.doi.org/10.1037/0003-066X.34.10.932
Amos, A. (2010) *Doubt, Conviction and the Analytic Process*. London: Routledge.
Berk, L. (2015) *Child Development*. London: Allyn & Bacon.

Bott, E. S., Milton, J., Garvey, P., Couve, C. and Steiner, D. (2011) *The New Dictionary of Kleinian Thought*. London: Routledge.

Bowlby, J. (1951) Maternal care and mental health. *World Health Organization Monograph Series*, 2: 179.

Bowlby, J. (1953) *Childcare and the Growth of Love*. Harmondsworth: Penguin.

Bowlby, J. (1958) The nature of the child's tie to his mother. *International Journal of Psychoanalysis*, 39, 350–371.

Bowlby, J. (1969) *Attachment. Attachment and Loss: Vol. 1. Loss*. New York: Basic Books.

Bowlby, J. (1982) Attachment and loss: Retrospect and prospect. *American journal of Orthopsychiatry*, 52 (4), 664–678.

Bowlby, R. (2019) *Fifty Years of Attachment Theory: The Donald Winnicott Memorial Lecture*. The Donald Winnicott Memorial Lecture Series. London: Routledge.

Clarke, G. S. (2018) *Fairbairn and the Object Relations Tradition*. London: Routledge.

Degotardi, S. and Pearson, E. (2014) *The Relationship Worlds of Infants and Toddlers*. Maidenhead: Open University Press.

Dollard, J. and Miller, N. (1950) *Personality and Psychotherapy*. New York: McGraw-Hill.

Dozier, M., Pelos, E., Lindhiem, O., Gordon, K., and Manni, M. (2006) Developing evidence-based interventions for foster children: An example of a randomized clinical trial with infants and toddlers. *Journal of Social Issues*, 62 (4): 767–785. https://doi.org/10.1111/j.1540-4560.2006.00486.x

Fairbairn, W. R. D. (1952) *Psycho-analytic Studies of the Personality*. London: Tavistock.

Fairbairn, W. R. D. (1956) A critical evaluation of certain basic psycho-analytical conceptions. *British Journal for the Philosophy of Science*, 7: 49–80.

Freud, A. (1966) A short history of child analysis. *Psychoanalytic Study of the Child*, 21: 7–14.

Graham, P. (2009) *Susan Isaacs: A Life Freeing the Minds of Children*. London: Routledge.

Greenberg, J. (1983) *Object Relations in Psychoanalytic Theory*. Cambridge, MA: Harvard University Press.

Harlow, H. F. (1981) The development of affectional patterns in infant monkeys. In B. M. Foss (ed.), *Determinants of Infant Behaviour*. New York: Wiley, 75–97.

Harlow, H. F. and Zimmermann, R. R. (1959) Affectional responses in the infant monkey. *Science*, 130, 421–432.

Isaacs, S. (1921) *Introduction to Psychology*. London: Methuen Press.

Isaacs, S. (1930) *The Intellectual Growth of Young Children*. London: Routledge & Kegan Paul.

Isaacs, S. (1940) Temper tantrums in early childhood in their relation to internal objects. *International Journal of Psychoanalysis*, 21: 280–293.

Isaacs, S. (1948) The nature and function of phantasy. *International Journal of Psychoanalysis*, 29: 73–97.

Kelly, A. (2023) Who was Anna Freud? *Better Help*, August 6. Available at: www.betterhelp.com/advice/psychologists/who-was-anna-freud/ (accessed September 29, 2023).

King, P. and Steiner, R. (1991) *The Freud–Klein Controversies 1941–1945*. New York: Routledge.

Klein, M. (1932/1997) *The Psychoanalysis of Children*. London: Vintage Books.

Klein, M. (1927) The psychological principles of infant analysis. *International Journal of Psychoanalysis*, 8: 25–37.

Klein, M. (1929) Personification in the play of children. *International Journal of Psychoanalysis*, 10: 193–204.

Klein, M. (1940) Mourning and its relation to manic-depressive states. *International Journal of Psychoanalysis*, 21, 125–153.

Klein, M. (1962) *Narrative of a Child Analysis*. New York: Basic Books.

Klein, M. (1997) *The Psycho-Analysis of Children*. London: Vintage.

Klein, M. (1998) *Love, Guilt and Reparation*. London: Vintage.

Klein, M., Heimann, P., Isaacs, S. and Riviere, J. (1952) *Developments in Psychoanalysis*. London: Hogarth.

Kohut, H. (1971) *The Analysis of the Self: A Systematic Approach to the Psychoanalytic Treatment of Narcissistic Personality Disorders*. New York: International Universities Press.

Mahler, M., Pine, F., and Bergman, A. (1975) *The Psychological Birth of the Human Infant*. New York: Basic Books.

Main, M. and Solomon, J. (1986) Discovery of an insecure-disorganized/disoriented attachment pattern. In T. B. Brazelton and M. W. Yogman (eds), *Affective Development in Infancy*. New York: Ablex Publishing, 95–124.

Mitchell, S. A. and Black, M. J. (1995) *Freud and Beyond: A History of Modern Psychoanalytic Thought*. London: Basic Books.

Parker, S. (2008) Winnicott's object relations theory and the work of the holy spirit. *Journal of Psychology and Theology*, 36 (4): 285–293. Available at: https://journals.sagepub.com/doi/pdf/10.1177/009164710803600404?casa_token=FGnsXbjD0EcAAAAA:gWJOfy9m3ab8ruza6ljK15h_5vsfDs3NXvwQFvykADnPjP3OxURPUS2eeZqSFhlPmRwyZKhd6cM

Pikler, E. (1972) Data on gross motor development of the infant. *Early Child Development and Care*, 1 (3): 297–310.

Rutter, M. (2002) Nature, nurture and development: From evangelism, through science towards policy and practice. *Child Development*, 73 (1): 1–21.

Sandler, A. (2015) *Anna Freud*. The Institute of Psychoanalysis. Available at: https://psychoanalysis.org.uk/our-authors-and-theorists/anna-freud (accessed September 29, 2023).

Sarner, M. (2018) Still have your childhood teddy? The psychological power of the toys we keep. *The Guardian*, December 12. Available at: www.theguardian.com/society/2018/dec/12/still-have-childhood-teddy-psychological-power-toys-we-keep (accessed September 29, 2023).

Schaffer, H. and Emerson, P. (1964) The development of social attachments in infancy. *Monographs of the Society for Research in Child Development*, 29 (3): 1–77.

Schwartz, A. (2012) The transitional objects and self comfort. MentalHelp.net, April 23. Available at: www.mentalhelp.net/blogs/the-transitional-objects-and-self-comfort/ (accessed September 29, 2023).

Tankersley, D., Vonta, T., and Ionescu, M. (2015) Quality in early childhood settings: Universal values and cultural flexibility. *Early Childhood Matters*, 124: 78–81.

Winnicott, D. W. (1971a) *Playing and Reality*. London: Penguin Books.

Winnicott, D. W. (1971b) *Therapeutic Consultations in Child Psychiatry*. London: Hogarth Press and the Institute of Psychoanalysis.

Winnicott, D. W. (1987) *Infants and Their Mothers*. New York: Addison-Wesley Publishing.

Chapter 4

Transitional Objects
Parents, Personal to Public

This chapter will explore the primary carer and the experiences with their young children having Transitional Objects (TO) in the 21st century. It will further develop parenting approaches and cultural attitudes about 'chosen' TO in private and public spaces, from home to settings. Attention will be given to the value of TO within families and their purpose from the child's and parents' perspective. Transitional Objects will be explored in relation to the importance of parent relationships and how humans and non-humans interact. The role of the professional is focused on the areas to reflect on regarding TO – the use of dummies, thumb sucking, and sleep time. The chapter ends with thinking about how working together in the parent–professional relationship can be achieved in the interest of the healthy development of the child.

Winnicott and Transitional Objects (TO)

Parenting is a significant transition and shift in a person's life and, as Knott (2019) confirms, considering 'mother' as a verb encapsulates the role they play, from having been a woman and now applying themselves to their baby's needs. Becoming established together requires confidence that she and her baby are suitably equipped to survive and thrive and in her own ability to provide what is needed to function.

Parenting can be viewed as both pleasure and pain with the quality and unique intensity experienced by the transition. Awareness of the potentials as a parent as well as the fears about their inadequacies come to the surface as the new-found space with an infant is navigated. This may evoke conscious or unconscious fears about doing harm and Winnicott described this period as Primary Maternal Preoccupation. The mother's needs and the baby's needs are so intimately linked that they are inseparable to the extent that he states there is no such thing as a baby ... if you set out to describe a baby, you will find you are describing a baby *and someone.* A baby cannot exist alone, but is essentially part of a relationship (Winnicott, 1964: 88).

DOI: 10.4324/9781003296669-6

Initially, the child is fused to the mother in a state of psychological symbiosis. As the baby matures, their development enables them to explore their environment. This involves a distancing from the mother, although this can be challenging for the child because of their deep attachment. Initially, the baby resolves this by alternating between moving away from her and checking back to ensure that she is still there – the mother being a secure base. Failure to offer this stable base creates a fear of its disappearance, forcing the child to physically cling to the mother, in case she might vanish. Separation anxiety is therefore considered a normal stage of development for babies at around 8 to 14 months, according to Bowlby (1979), but can also occur at different times in a young child's life. The baby will become distressed when their parent goes out of view or leaves the room. The feelings are tied up with a very real fear that their parent or trusted adult will go away and not come back. By the time a child reaches the age of about two, children begin to feel safe and independent in other environments. 'Children are able to recognise that, although parents may temporarily leave them with other people, they do return' (PACEY, 2014: 5).

La Leche League (LLL) believes that the presence of the mother is as important for the child as her milk and many mothers who attend LLL groups co-sleep with their babies and toddlers and minimize separation wherever possible. It would seem plausible, then, to consider that babies of mothers who practice attachment parenting would not need attachment objects, or as Winnicott defines, 'transitional objects', due to their mothers being ever present.

> At school once my daughter's teacher was asking them about special teddies that helped them get to sleep and she told her that she had always had her mummy and didn't need a teddy.
>
> (Allan, 2017)

However, different children have different needs for internal and external comfort as well as varied and complex environments and the relationships within it. An infant having a close attachment with their mother does not assume that TO wouldn't feature in their lives. And while some researchers have suggested there is no correlation between a child's tendency to have a TO and their attachment to their mothers (Van IJzendoorn et al., 1983), others have suggested the contrary, concluding that the less attached a child is to their mother, the more likely they may be to have an attachment object. What is confirmed is that babies and children (even us adults) benefit from all forms of physical touch, from birth to childhood (Allan, 2017). Transitional objects are more broadly transitional in the sense that they help the child to bridge the transition between caring experiences. They enable a needy or distressed or regressed child to manage the gap between direct caregiving experiences. That could mean helping a three-year-old tolerate falling asleep on her own in the family's new home, a five-year-old to manage the shift from one parent's care into the care of another, or a 12-year-old to walk through the door to their new classroom. Garber's (2019) study extended this by concluding how TO can assist children who are experiencing separation anxiety, when they are in child custody, following high conflict divorce. The study evaluated that the court has a responsibility to encourage litigating parents to respect the child's needs for TO alongside the human relationships offered.

Furthermore, Richins and Chaplin (2021) offer the concept of transitory object attachments, in which children quickly attach to an object but un-attach almost as quickly in early childhood and adulthood. While many object attachments are beneficial in the long term, transitory attachments can in some cases be harmful to children. This, for example, occurs when mobiles or videogames become addictive. It can also occur when transitory attachments become counterproductive; for example, when children rely too heavily on objects to perform developmental tasks such as developing a sense of self and gaining the respect of others. Whilst beyond the scope of the book it is worth considering how TO are reflected on beyond infancy and early childhood.

Object Relations theory explains both how the body contributes to psychological development and how body image disturbance can develop because of a person's early psychological history. Based on extensive observation of children, Margaret Mahler and colleagues proposed a phase theory of human development in which the body image starts to form from the very beginning of life, in the interaction between the child and the mother. Fundamentally, the mother's physical handling creates physical sensations that literally form the reality of the body as being a separate entity from the outside world. It is their hands on the child's body that convey for the child the very first sense of their physical existence with boundaries (Mahler, Pine and Bergman, 2008).

Voice Vignette: Infant Massage and Therapeutic Touch

Family Hubs in the UK (Hayes, 2021) have many programmes to support the parent–infant relationship. One such programme is the International Association of Infant Massage (IAIM) which focuses on touch and bonding.

Question to Consider

In creating opportunities for loving touch, consider how the IAIM supports communication, attachment and why do they consider asking the infant permission to be touched?

Think about the considerations about:

- Respect.
- Voice.
- Listening and taking the lead from the infant's cues.
- Developing a sense of separateness from the parent.

Separation and the Transitional Object (TO)

For an infant to be able to explore further they may need to mentally represent their parent and in resolving this the infant may adopt an object that has 'mother-like' properties. This TO is usually soft, malleable, and fragrant with the smell of the mother. It is also invested with the capacity to perform for the child the psychological functions that the mother thus far provided, such as emotional support and reassurance. Winnicott (1953), further elaborated the role of the TO in psychological development. They suggested that the first TO is the child's body, as it is the first vehicle through which the child experiences sensations from the mother. Contact with one's own body can therefore serve a transitional function by evoking contact with the mother (Applegate, 1989).

However, as the child matures and becomes more involved with their external world, objects become used as TO. The adoption of external TO replaces the embodied experience of the mother (or main carer) with the beginning of a mental representation of them that, at this point, still requires the concrete support of an actual physical object. According to Winnicott (1953), in the first months of life, thanks to the maternal attention and care the child receives, they imagine that they and their mother are one and the same person. However as previously discussed, the child soon learns that there is a division as well as a realisation that their mother (or main carer) is not always present to satisfy their needs, resulting in seeking an object for this transition phase, especially at times such as bedtime. This period may last for a short or long period. The child may also need the TO while at other times appearing to discard it. This may be because the child needs to live several situations directing love, care, aggression, and even hatred to this object, as a learning process by the child, with the growing knowledge of being capable in surviving without it. The process is navigated by the child and whilst some may not become attached to any TO, others seem dependent on them (A Matter of Style, 2022).

As the child further matures and needs psychological support, they will be able to evoke an internalised, well-represented object and experience its comfort.

In general, the development of object relations is viewed as going through three main stages:

1   an undifferentiated or objectless stage;
2   a transitional stage;
3   a stage of object relations.

Although object relations theory holds some resemblance to attachment theory, the empirical status of the latter is much more elaborated. Attachment theoretical concepts are informed and influenced from ethology, psychoanalysis, cognitive psychology, and systems theory. Of particular importance is the impact of care givers' behaviour and attitude.

Caregiving that promotes secure mother–infant attachments includes characteristics such as sensitivity, positive attitude, synchrony, mutuality, support, and stimulation (Kernberg, 2001).

Voice Vignettes: Consider the Following Scenarios and Reflect on Where Comfort Objects Fit into Attachment Parenting?

I used to have a monkey and I couldn't get to sleep without him. Eventually he lost both his eyes. And his fur was damaged by an orange-juice spill and had to be replaced. But I loved him anyway. My own children have a dog, a lamb, and a bear (Ralphs, 2023).

As a caring approach to overcome initial feelings of insecurity and come to terms with separation from and the absence of their parents, familiar photos or a book are objects children can bring to the setting as a reminder of home (PACEY, 2014). Laminated photos attached to a key ring for the child to hold or have attached to clothing are further ways children can connect with home (Allan, 2019, n.p.).

Consider the Following Scenario and Reflect on Where Do Comfort Objects Fit into Attachment Parenting?

My favourite childhood toy was a puffin (actually he still is). He was given to me when I was two and quickly usurped a boss-eyed white bear to which I had previously been attached. I was faithful only to Puffin throughout my childhood and into my teens. Although I now live in Central Asia, he lives (and I use the word intentionally) at my parents' house in England. When I go back, much to my husband's ridicule, he often shares my bed. I find the presence of my puffin as comforting as I always did. He represents a continuum in my life. Of course, I don't really attribute any independent life force to him – he is a tatty stuffed toy with a beak made from an old sweater. But he represents safety and love and has a powerful effect on my stress levels (Allan, 2017, n.p.).

Attitudes towards TO and Connecting Them to Relationships and Theories during the 20th Century

In Western culture it was only in the 1950s that comfort objects began to be recognised as a positive presence in a child's life. Until that time, prevailing child care practices stressed baby's early independence and regarded attachment to an object as a deficiency in the child, or a kind of strange fetish, attention seeking, or the charm of being a child and the toys that accompanied them (Wulff, 1946). Moreover, a baby's instinctive attachment to their mother was considered a biological need for food and warmth. Winnicott's (1953) work, 'Transitional objects and transitional phenomena: a study of the first not-me possession' speaks of comfort objects as a familiar aspect of childhood development, which play a part in the child's growing independence from its mother. The toy or blanket serving to represent the mother when they are not there enables the child to manage stress and have the confidence to explore the environment. Transitional objects connect with Winnicott's theory of 'the good-enough mother', sensitively preparing the baby for the outside world by not being everything, always. Winnicott sees the key role of the 'good-enough' mother as providing the comfort of being connected with the mother. This 'holding environment' allows the infant to transition at its own rate to a more autonomous position. He sees the micro-interactions between the mother and child as central to the development of the internal world. After the early stage of connection with the mother and illusions of omnipotence comes the stage of 'relative dependence', where they realise their dependence and learn about loss. By moving away from the child in well-timed small doses, the mother helps develop a healthy sense of independence. Her failure to adapt to every need of the child helps them adapt to external realities. Three key aspects of the environment identified by Winnicott are holding, handling, and object-presenting. The mother may thus hold the child, handle it, and present objects to it, whether it is herself, her breast, or a separate object (Winnicott, 1992). The good enough mother will do this to the general satisfaction of the child. By not being perfect, he writes, the good-enough mother gradually loosens the holding of the baby, rather than dropping it suddenly (Winnicott, 2016). In the 1960s, attachment theory also promoted the idea that children use objects of security such as blankets as a calming substitute for their key attachment figure, and by the 1970s, eminent child care writers like Dr Spock and Penelope Leach were actively advocating the introduction of comfort objects to help young children manage times of separation. Objects that are infused with the powerful essence of mother, babyhood, protection, and safety cannot comfortably be shared, washed, or left behind (Brenner, 2004).

In understanding the value placed on TO further, the following case study is a prime example of how they continue to be significant in the 21st century. In using social media as a form of communication, a mother discusses her daughter's feelings of loss when her TO goes missing. It is powerful example of the ripple effect TO has, not only on the children themselves but also on those close relationships around them – the TO becoming significant and having meaning for the parent as much as the child.

Voice Vignette: This Is the Story of Bunny, the Love and Loss of a Transitional Object

Bunny was not a fictional thing but a real-life TO that was missed by its child and parent. The following illustration highlights how we feel as a parent in trying to 'hold' our child and emotionally support them through their lived experiences.

The Mothers' Narrative

In despair, no tears, just conviction that Bunny would come back, we went back to Birmingham, UK, to search for Bunny. We asked in every café, the library, the station, the university, the history department to keep an eye out for Bunny.

To start with we had to retell our child that Bunny was gone, lost. She refused to sleep with any other softie. Bunny was her favourite. Only Bunny would do. When she saw other favourite softies on television, she went quiet. She woke up in the night. She occasionally said she misses Bunny.

We despaired and we made a card for the fairies, asking them to search for Bunny. They say they will send one back, along with fairy dust saying they would look.

She just crawls up into herself.

She sometimes acknowledges that she misses Bunny as the days and weeks pass.

We finally convinced her that Bunny was not coming back, and that old Bunny was gone.

She howled then.

We asked her if she might like the moon fairy to bring her a moon Bunny. Not her Bunny exactly but a similar Bunny.

She said yes.

We now have a whole back story about the moon fairy!

We couldn't find any kids stories that didn't have closure where the last toy was never found.

Today the moon fairy delivered. The arrival was a little pink moon Bunny.

All the love that was reserved for Bunny is finally being transferred to this fluffier and pinker soft toy.

It is a love I haven't seen in a month and a month is a long time with a little person.

We did have a spare bunny, but she could always tell the difference. It was called baby back-up Bunny but was never a substitute for true Bunny.

Response to the narrative: I have had a few such losses and emotional journeys as a child. I still treasure the ones I have but sometimes I wonder about my toy's journey after I left him in the sand dunes …

A Last Note

On the Bunny situation … My little one still says she misses old Bunny, although she sleeps much better now that she has her moon bunny. Last night she told her Mumma that when she's sad about old Bunny she doesn't want moon bunny. She said that the moon fairy changed old Bunny into moon bunny, so maybe the moon fairy can change moon bunny back into old Bunny. We have denied this, but I still wonder where that little old Bunny is … So sad! (shared by Onni Gust, 2023, personal communication).

Gust was an oral contributor who kindly allowed me to share this story, which she had posted on social media, and for me it resonated on so many levels. One area as an educator that I was left pondering about was:

We couldn't find any kids stories that didn't have closure where the last toy was never found.

An important area to reflect on and in discussing this I think it is often our own desire to make things 'right' and to protect our children, but we are not always able to resolve the things our children need. How, therefore, do we enable resilience to grow and sensitively support children in closure when the last toy is not found? For me, Gust achieved this through talking and being led by the child but also observing the child's behaviour and being attuned to their feelings.

Replacing a loved object is challenging. In an experiment, scientists tricked small children into thinking their toys had been cloned in a special machine. With the strongly attached children, four refused to have their object copied at all, and of the 18 who did, 13 unsurprisingly refused a seemingly identical substitute. If the loved object does, as many believe, represent their mother, their acceptance would have meant taking in a substitute mother, one that is identical in looks but unknown and instinctively flawed in essence (Hood and Bloom, 2008, cited in Hartley, Fisher, and Fletcher, 2020).

Voice Vignette: Cat

This was fascinating and resonated with my own experiences as a professional and parent, trying to substitute a cat that was temporarily lost. My daughter, even with a new sewed brooch never really accepted new cat and when the old one turned up it again took centre stage.

Here Is the Story of the Cat

The cat was introduced to Alex when he was one year old and had begun attending a singing class. He had been given it alongside several other toys. This was in July, and he would snuggle into it and hold it close but wasn't observed to have a particular love for it, with other cuddly blankets and teddies being used as well. In September his parent began a new job and Alex began nursery. The mother would leave the house at 5:15 am and dad would take him to the nursery and pick him up. His mum would return later around 6:30 pm and this was a regular occurrence three days a week. During this time, it was observed that the soft cuddly cat was being singled out from a collection of other toys. The cat would be pulled and cuddled and was often carried by its fur. The cat was requested by Alex, and he hugged it closely to his body during the transition from home to nursery. Sometimes he would grab it, sometimes he would bite it, and sometimes he would pull it. One morning he had woken up early and as his mum was leaving; she recalled seeing him at the window crying for her and not wanting her to leave. She had called once from work and Dad said he had settled and had been cuddling his cat as he was helped to get dressed and given breakfast. The cat became an extension of Alex as the first not me possession. He had used it as a symbol of the separation between his parents as well as the transition to nursery school. The nursery staff allowed the cat to remain with him and it became part of his play and represented part of his family and himself.

As Alex grew, he had a sibling, a sister; as she turned three years old, she too had decided the cat was very much part of her world. By this time Alex was six years old and for him the cat, although it remained a sentimental toy, had lost its urgency with him, and he didn't feel or seem to have the desire to keep it with him. His sister, Octavia, however, would use the cat as a comfort to sleep and transition to the nursery as well. Her mother had noted by this stage the stuffing had gone and the cat was looking very tatty and very worn. On Octavia's birthday she decided she would buy the same cat, from the same shop, but customise it with a bow and make it special for Octavia rather than a hand-me-down toy of her brother's. The new cat arrived, firm and upright, stuffing bulging out its limbs (Figure 4.1).

The new cat was accepted, but slowly the older cat was preferred, wrapped in arms close to her body with the new cat often found on the floor. The TO, the older cat, had lived through two siblings' needs and had seemed to have a purpose as a source of comfort for them both, whilst the two cats coexisted in the here and now. The observations are a gentle reminder how lost and replaced objects may never quite meet the child's total acceptance and emotional needs as the original object had.

Figure 4.1 Alex and his TO cat, giving it a squeeze. This was taken as he was waiting for his mum to pick him up from the day care setting. His facial expression looks quite serious, nervous perhaps, and he is hunched over his objects.

Whilst the children are older now, the cats remain in the bedroom and I recently compared the two, six months apart in age when purchased, both now over ten years old. Observing the images, you can visibly observe the one that was the TO and the other the replacement cat (Figure 4.2).

This also reminded me of Philo's (2018) example of the account of teddy explored in Chapter 1.

> Teddy I no longer live with Teddy. He decided to stay at my parents' house when I went to university, probably because he is a creature of haunts and habits. Teddy – for that is his unimaginative name – was not my original teddy, and he always struggled to fill the role vacated by his predecessor, also called Teddy, who was left on a train when I was very young. Original Teddy, even now, possibly retains a higher place in my affections than replacement Teddy: the former really was my most crucial 'transitional object' as I grew.
>
> (Philo, 2018)

The predecessor, still significant but in a different way and often relegated to the home, was needed less as the transitional spaces took place. Consideration of the TO and the shifting of child behaviours is also helpful to reflect on the parents' contributing efforts to their child having a TO as they move from their own bodily sensory experiences to including an external object as part of their every day.

Thumb Sucking and Modern-day Comforters, Bottle and Dummies

As a psychoanalyst, Winnicott evaluated that thumb sucking, which he termed oral erotism, is often associated with genital self-stimulation (masturbation). In

Figure 4.2 TO cat and toy cat together and the difference is telling, with one leaning over and the other upright.

the late 1870s, thumb sucking was mentioned in the literature of diseases of children. By 1910, paediatric textbooks referred to thumb sucking as a disease and this remained until the mid-twentieth century (Candlin and Guins, 2009).

As the child sucks their thumb, they often take an external object such as a blanket, part of a sheet, or a handkerchief into the mouth using the other hand. The child then sucks the cloth or smells it or rubs it against the cheek.

The texture and smell are important for going to sleep and as a defence against anxiety. Washing the TO may change its smell or texture in ways that the child finds unacceptable. Winnicott describes how the infant assumes the rights over the TO, cuddled affectionately one moment, loved excitedly, or mutilated at different times, and needs to survive this loving and hating. It must never change unless at the infant's instigation. Winnicott states that, although the child does not see it as coming from within, they know it is not a hallucination, it is real. Winnicott believes the TO supports the infant and young child to distinguish what is part of the mother (the breast or total maternal care), part of the baby (the thumb), and what is external (the object) (Isaacs and Isaacs, 2014).

However, many parents may have concerns that their five-year-old cannot sleep without their dummy or their teenager will refuse to throw out the tattered blanket they have had since they were a child. A need for comfort is part of being human, and comfort objects remind us of feeling calm, secure, and loved. They are the bridge that links between a new situation and the comfort of home. Although research in the 1940s considered such items a sign of poor attachment, Winnicott later proposed that they were in fact the opposite. Rather than being an object to turn to in lieu of love and care, they were a reminder of love and security. A study found that kids with strong bonds to TO have stronger attachment to a parent and are happier than those without.

Some comfort objects, however, are deemed culturally and even physically preferable to others. The evidence for using dummies (pacifiers) or bottles after twelve months of age is less positive. Similarly, although babies thumb suck in the womb, and babies are born with an innate need to suck, thumb sucking is often discouraged in certain cultures. Breastfeeding and sucking calms them and increases the mother's milk supply. Dummies can help bottle-fed babies to suck and calm themselves. Sometimes breastfeeding mums use them, but if a baby meets its sucking needs elsewhere, there is the concern that this can potentially reduce the milk supply, so they aren't recommended in the first six weeks. The subject of whether to give a baby a dummy or not can be divisive. If used carefully, they can have some benefits for young babies and are recommended at night as they have been found to reduce the risk of sudden infant death syndrome, possibly because they stop a baby sleeping too deeply. Whitmarsh (2008) evaluated the use of pacifiers in formal day care and offered a valuable example to the discourses associated with certain practices, how parental rights and their own ambivalent views can contradict authoritative knowledge, and how this is managed in early years settings (Norman, 2019). She concluded that professionals considered the pacifier to be harmful to communication, generally due to observations and advice from speech and language therapists, alongside personal views of them being unhygienic and impractical in a group setting. However, they continued to use them and followed parental advice rather than professional advice. In the study the practitioners had limited knowledge of the benefits of using pacifiers as a possible prevention of sudden infant death syndrome (SIDS), and one practitioner voiced the contradictory advice to her own existing perceptions of the negative impact of using pacifiers by the media. The study highlighted the everyday complexities of parental choice, group care, and tensions between practitioners and care practices. Comforters come in a variety of forms and have been used for many years and, specifically, pacifiers or dummies as they are commercially known, remain less researched as a care practice. These are sucking tools in a bid to calm and self-comfort, a TO, with the comfort objects as a way for children to calm and soothe themselves (Brown, 2018).

Cultural Sleep, Lullabies, and TO

Ways of supporting sleep have predominately been anecdotal from family members and friends, alongside professional guidance, imparting appropriate ways to encourage sleep. Currently, the overall message is that infants should be sleeping in the presence of a significant adult in the first six months. Falling asleep in psychological terms means losing control of reality and plunging into a world of fantasy with the potential anguish experienced by an infant when he shuts his eyes and consequently loses control of external reality. As the child experiences the separation from their parent, an object soon becomes indispensable for them and as a valuable mother substitute. They are important, not only at bedtime but also whenever the child feels lonely, sad, and depressed. They are considered a Talisman, and many parents intuitively recognise the value of the possession and keep the objects handy for moments of tension, avoiding even washing them so as not to modify their global sensory configuration.

Transitional phenomena are important in thinking about the space and time at bedtime with the object. This is the intermediate space symbolising the protective reunion with mothers. Other symbolic ways children seek comfort is by rocking and swaying in the arms of their parent. Frequently rocking infants in arms or in the cradle can support them as they transition to sleep. Lullabies or nursery rhymes or even a prayer may also be an accompaniment with other comforting behaviour, as the child separates from the outside world. Historically, using lullabies and nursery rhymes in supporting an infant to going to sleep is not a new concept. Friedrich Froebel's (1782–1852) philosophy of education was unique in that he advocated mutual respect and holistic learning. He promoted learning through experience and considered Mother Songs/Lullabies to be the initial stage in developing early physical skills of the body and senses. The print culture of the 18th century was overlaying the oral tradition of verse, capturing a wealth of traditional nursery rhymes such as the lullaby's nonsense and playground rhymes. *The Mother Song Book* (Froebel, 1879), a family book, addressed its readership to the mother alone but in the last chapter to both mother and father. It developed the relationship between parent and infant within the family context, with a reciprocal communication, gaining a sense of belonging to their family, community, and culture. Froebel considered Mother Songs as a way of forming close supporting emotional relationships through actively engaging. The significance of this was his emphasis on creating care connections with the whole family, educators, and the community. He also focused on the importance for infants to be able to move their body, limbs, hands, and fingers, introducing educational movement games with children who were able to walk and talk (Bruce, 2012). The purpose was also for the mother to gain a sense of rewarding responsibility in supporting the development of their infant in their care (Bruce, 2012, 2021).

> Indeed, man's whole development requires that his surroundings speak to him clearly ... So in words and songs the mother tries to express this and bring the life of his environment closer to him.
>
> (Froebel in Lilley, 1967: 105)

A Froebelian philosophy engaging in The Mother Songs principles and pedagogy included:

- Recognition of the uniqueness of each child's capacity and potential.
- A holistic approach to learning which recognises children as active, feeling, and thinking human beings, seeing patterns and making connections.
- Individual and collaborative activity and play (Norman, 2019; Tovey, 2012).

Included in the Mother Songs were finger rhymes which involved musical voice alongside finger manipulation moving in unique ways.

> Music is especially important, since the sounds which a child produces in singing ... serve to give creative expression to feelings and ideas.
>
> (Froebel in Lilley, 1967: 113)

The rocking, singing, and nursery rhymes are all implicit in helping the child fall asleep in the absence of their TO, or in reflecting about this further, the songs themselves can be the TO, the words, the rhythm, and the sleep space, the cradle or cot.

In the fear of being abandoned, the infant seeks comfort by being rocked and preferably maintaining direct contact with the mother's body as they fall asleep. In many countries the child simply goes to bed while being carried on the mother's back. This reunion can take place in a less concrete fashion without physical contact, by means of a lullaby. The movement and contact with her body has the same value as an inanimate object which establishes it as a bridge between me and not me, between internal and external reality. The TO is distinct and separate from their mother's body. Therefore, it is the first attempt to establish a relationship with the outside world.

The lullaby song in the cradle or bed lies halfway between a TO and being rocked in the arms. Between approximately eight months and the end of the second year, the infant must possess an object capable of symbolising their reunion with their mother that belongs to the earliest period of care experienced as a part of the mother and, as such, invested in trust.

Working Together to Support Parents

Entering parenthood is of course an exciting and sacred time for many, a gratifying and wonderous experience of being able to raise a family. However, the pandemic and beyond has increasingly revealed the complex tensions of caring for infants during their first 1001 days, in certain circumstances and at certain times. Research and policy reveal some of these troubling narratives around parenthood through their experiences. An ideology of women as natural mothers, immediately able to care for their babies, and ultimately fulfilled in this role of selfless carer and nurturer is a far cry from many new parents' reality, both historically and in the present day. Most individuals experience varying degrees of anxiety; it is a natural human state and a vital part of everyday living. Anxiety helps identify and respond to danger in 'fight or flight' mode. It can be a motivating feeling, enabling an individual to face and deal with difficult challenges. The 'right' amount of anxiety can help individuals perform better, stimulating action and creativity. Nevertheless, persistent anxiety causes emotional distress and leads to a feeling of being unwell and, at worst, developing anxiety disorders (Mental Health Foundation, 2023).

A way forward in improving mental well-being and promoting good mental health is enabling new parents to retain autonomy and have agency of voice. By being able to share their emotional states, including their fears, concerns, and aspirations within a community about their transitioning role to parenthood, they can navigate their journey with support from professionals, seeking help where necessary. Transitioning to fatherhood has to a lesser extent been researched during and beyond the pandemic (Fatherhood Institute, 2021a).

In supporting the mental well-being of new dads, the Fatherhood Institute and Mental Health Foundation published *Becoming Dad*, a new guide for expectant and new fathers, launched in November 2021. They consider there is still a real lack of well-written, evidence-based information designed specifically to help men navigate their personal journeys into fatherhood. This matters not just for the men themselves, but for the women who love them, and the babies they will father and be emotionally available for (Fatherhood Institute, 2021b). Winnicott (1951) described the holding environment as a safe environment that emotionally holds the baby through pain and uncertainty and complements the notion of 'containment' proposed by Bion (1962).

This concept has been widened to include the 'holding in mind' of others. Through these developing grass roots initiatives and projects there is increasing recognition of the various ways both partners can emotionally hold each other in supporting and caring for their child during their first 1001 days. By enabling parents to share their experiences, the projects have all evaluated the benefits parents felt in being heard and communicating in a way that may help others. Their authentic stories contribute to a widening call for maternal services that promote prevention and community outreach projects that rely predominately on charitable funds and would benefit from local government investment (Parent–Infant Foundation, 2022).

Gopnik (2017) argued that parenting in modern society assumes that the 'right' parenting techniques or expertise will shape an infant into a successful adult. Shaping a product is the method of a carpenter and, in referring to parenting, very little empirical evidence supports this approach. Gopnik concluded it is the small modifications in what parents do, as carers, that have reliable and long-term effects on who those infants and young children will become. For her, raising and caring for children is like tending a garden: it involves creating a safe, nurturing space in which innovation, adaptability, and resilience can thrive: good-enough parenting. Winnicott, as discussed, also recognised that children who had a 'good (enough) mother' could flourish and develop, despite a lack of hygiene and being exposed to poor physical conditions, often associated with families deemed to be living in poverty. It was the warmth of mothering, infants being carried, cooed to, as well as the sensory experience of skin-to-skin contact that contributed to the close relationship and thriving infant (Norman, 2019).

Summarising the Key Thoughts about Transitional Objects and Transitional Phenomena

The guiding principles of person-centred planning with parents is that:

- Parents are listened to, and their views and feeling are considered.
- Parents are valued partners who play an important role in making decisions.
- Autonomy is promoted and parents are empowered to develop a voice.
- A person-centred culture is developed and how this could be integrated into policies, attitudes, and daily practices is reflected on.

Parent, defined in its broadest sense, includes those carers who take the primary lead in the parenting role. No parent or family should be excluded from this process. Parents must feel included, listened to and trusted within their own role supporting their child's well-being, development, and learning. Each unique family must be welcomed and listened to. Central to this is valuing parents and carers as children's first educators and giving them the opportunity to contribute to the whole of their child's journey as the child attends formal day care (DfE, 2021: 28).

A Final Note

This chapter began with some further thinking about TO and how this can be used across childhood, from birth to adulthood. Examples of the value of TO were discussed, with the loss being long term and substitute TO never quite being the same. The latter part of the chapter closes with a reminder about the importance of parent relationships and how humans and non-humans interact. The role of the professional is focused on and the areas to reflect on regarding TO are the use of dummies, thumb sucking, and sleep time. This culminates in thinking about how working together as professionals with parents can be achieved in the interest of the healthy development of the child.

References

Allan, A. (2017) Cloth mothers: Where do comfort objects fit into attachment parenting? Personal blog. Available at: https://aliceallan.co.uk/2017/02/01/cloth-mothers-where-do-comfort-objects-fit-into-attachment-parenting/ (accessed October 2, 2023).

Allan, A. (2019) Comfort objects and attachment parenting. La Leche League International, 26 February. Available at: https://llli.org/comfort-objects-and-attachment-parenting/ (accessed October 2, 2023).

A Matter of Style (2022) How do transitional objects help children? May 6. Available at: www.amatterofstyle.eu/inspire-me/transitional-objects-children (accessed October 2, 2023).

Applegate, J. S. (1989) The transitional object reconsidered: Some sociocultural variations and their implications. *Child and Adolescent Social Work Journal*, 6: 38–51. https://doi.org/10.1007/BF00755709

Bion, W. R. (1962) The psycho-analytic study of thinking. *International Journal of Psychoanalysis*, 43 (4–5): 306–310.

Bowlby, J. (1979) The Bowlby–Ainsworth attachment theory. *Behavioral and Brain Sciences*, 2 (4): 637–638.

Brenner, M. (2004) *Pacifiers, Blankets and Bottles*. New York: Simon & Schuster.

Brown, A. (2018) From dummies to blankies – when should you worry about your child's attachment to comfort items? Available at: www-2018.swansea.ac.uk/press-office/news-archive/2018/fromdummiestoblankieswhenshouldyouworryaboutyourchildsattachmenttocomfortitems.php#acceptFrom%20dummies%20to%20blankies%20%E2%80%93%20when%20should%20you%20worry%20about%20your%20child%E2%80%99s%20attachment%20to%20comfort%20items?

Bruce, T. (2012) *Early Childhood Practice: Froebel Today*. London: Sage Publications.

Bruce, T. (2021) *Froebel*. London: Bloomsbury.

Candlin, F. and Guins, R. (2009) *The Object Reader*. London: Routledge.

Department for Education (2021) Birth to 5 Matters. Available at: Birthto5Matters. org.uk, p. 28.

Fatherhood Institute (2021a) Becoming dad. October 21, 2021. Available at: www.fa therhoodinstitute.org/2021/becoming-dad/ (accessed October 2, 2023).

Fatherhood Institute (2021b) Dads shut out: Fathers and maternity services during the pandemic. 19 November. Available at: www.fatherhoodinstitute.org/2021/dads-shu t-out-fathers-and-maternity-services-during-the-pandemic/ (accessed October 2, 2023).

Froebel, F. (1879) *Mother-play and Nursery Songs: With Notes to Mothers* (Transla-tion). London: Lee & Shepard.

Garber, B. (2019) For the love of fluffy: Respecting, protecting, and empowering Transitional Objects in the context of high-conflict divorce. *Journal of Divorce & Remarriage*, 60 (7): 552–565. https://doi.org/10.1080/10502556.2019.1586370

Gopnik, A. (2017) *The Gardener and the Carpenter: What the New Science of Infant Development Tells Us about the Relationship between Parents and Children*. London: Vintage.

Hartley, C., Fisher, S., and Fletcher, S. (2020) Exploring the influence of ownership history on object valuation in typical development and autism. *Cognition*, 197, 104187. https://doi.org/10.1016/j.cognition.2020.104187

Hayes, D. (2021) Family hubs: Five key questions. *Children and Young People Now Select*, 11: 15–15.

Isaacs, D. and Isaacs, S. (2014) Transitional objects. *Journal of Paediatrics and Child Health*, 50: 845–846. https://doi.org/10.1111/jpc.12747

Kernberg, O. F. (2001) *International Encyclopedia of the Social & Behavioral Sciences*. Available at: www.sciencedirect.com/referencework/9780080430768/internationa l-encyclopedia-of-the-social-and-behavioral-sciences (accessed October 2, 2023).

Knott, S. (2019) *Mother*. London: Penguin Books.

Lilley, I. (1967) *Friedrich Froebel: A Selection from His Writings*. Cambridge: Cam-bridge University Press.

Mahler, M. S., Pine, F., and Bergman, A. (2008) *The Psychological Birth of the Human Infant: Symbiosis and Individuation*. London: Basic Books.

Mental Health Foundation (2023) Anxiety. Available at: www.mentalhealth.org.uk/ sites/default/files/living-with-anxiety-report.pdf (accessed October 2, 2023).

Norman, A. (2019) *From Conception to Two: Development, Policy and Practice*. London: Routledge.

PACEY (2014) Transitions and settling in: A guide to help you think about how you can support the transitions and settling in processes that the children in your care experience. Available at: www.pacey.org.uk/Pacey/media/Website-files/school%20rea dy/PG10-transitions-and-settling-in.pdf (accessed October 2, 2023).

Parent–Infant Foundation (2022) First 1001 days movement. Available at: https://pa rentinfantfoundation.org.uk/1001-days/ (accessed October 2, 2023).

Philo, C. (2018) When teddy met teddie. *Children's Geographies*, 16 (4): 455–458. https:// doi.org/10.1080/14733285.2018.1457754

Ralphs, A. (2023) What's your child's transitional object? Thread Bear Design, Feb-ruary 23, 2023. Available at: https://threadbeardesign.co.uk/blogs/news/wha ts-your-childs-transitional-object (accessed October 2, 2023).

Richins, M. and Chaplin, L. (2021) Object attachment, transitory attachment, and materialism in childhood. *Current Opinion in Psychology*, 39: 20–25.

Tovey, H. (2012) *Bringing the Frobel Approach to Your Early Years Setting*. London: Routledge.

Van IJzendoorn, M. H., Tavecchio, L. W. C., Goossens, F. A., Vergeer, M. M. and Swaan, J. (1983) How B is B4? Attachment and security of Dutch children in Ainsworth's strange situation and at home. *Psychological Reports*, 52: 683–691.

Whitmarsh, J. (2008) Mums, dummies and 'dirty dids': The dummy as a symbolic representation of mothering? *Children & Society*, 22: 278–290. https://doi.org/10. 1111/j.1099-0860.2007.00082.x

Winnicott, D. W. (1951) *Transitional Objects and Transitional Phenomena*. London: Tavistock.

Winnicott, D. W. (1953) Transitional objects and transitional phenomena: A study of the first not-me possession. *International Journal of Psychoanalysis*, 34: 89–97.

Winnicott, D. W. (1964) *The Child, the Family and the Outside World*. London: Pelican Books.

Winnicott, D. W. (1992) *Babies and Their Mothers*. London: Da Capo Press; reprint edition.

Winnicott, D. W. (2016) *The Collected Works of D. W. Winnicott* (Vol. 12). Oxford: Oxford University Press.

Wulff, M. (1946) Fetishism and object choice in early childhood. *The Psychoanalytic Quarterly*, 15: 450–471.

Part Two

Transitional Objects and Early Years Practice

Chapter 5

Transitions and Formal Day Care

Transitional Objects (TO) will be explored in relation to young children. The chapter will further examine the psychological and potential space TO have to offer. It will also include the sense of trust and independence when being alone and playing. Winnicott (1960/2018) theorised TO attachments and ego development leading to a sense of self. Additionally, the capacity for symbolisation, creativity, memory, empathy, and object relations are also weaved into the discussions. In drawing on empirical research, knowledge of TO will be further discussed, specifically its relevance in the 21st-century pandemic. Transitional times will be drawn on as examples to develop the discussion. This offers the TO as being purposefully relevant and serving a variety of psychological foundations as the child moves towards physical and emotional independence (Figure 5.1).

Attachment and Transitions

Attachment is central to a sense of security, leading to social competence and resilience. The ethological theory, developed by Bowlby (2005), is a widely an accepted view of attachment today, both in the family context and in the way

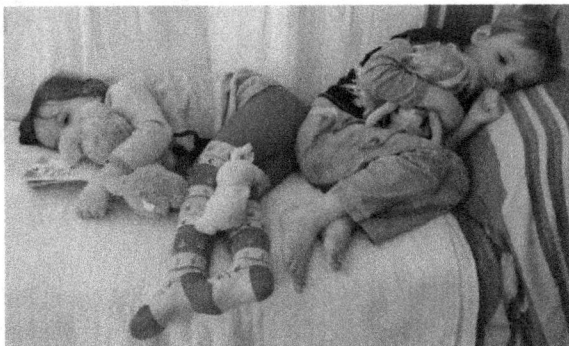

Figure 5.1 Transitional Objects and their relevance to early years practice.

DOI: 10.4324/9781003296669-8

practitioners look after children in formal day care within England (Barnes, 1995). Belsky et al. (2007) developed understandings of attachment to argue that it is not simply about a static single or stable relationship but rather the changes that occur within the relationships that evolve over time and are context dependent. Similarly, Dunn (Booth and Dunn, 1994) argued that mothers display different levels of bonding depending on the age of their child, and as the infant's independence develops in the first two years the intensity of the attachment lessens. However, although attachment is conceived as being fluid, particularly after the first year, primary attachments remain an important aspect in supporting the emotional development of young children (Barnes, 1995). The infant develops more complex understanding of the carers who look after them, within and beyond the home, and they begin to make assessments about the environmental situation, including their own role and the carer's role within it (Cooper and Roth, 2003).

Bowlby (1969) described the internal images or maps that are built up because of these exchanges as Internal Working Models (IWMs). These IWMs enable the child to anticipate and interpret the behaviour of other people and plan a response. Where the caregiver is experienced as a source of security and support, the child develops IWMs in which they have a positive self-image and in which other people are depicted as being trustworthy and responsive. Children with non-attuned or abusive caregivers internalise a less positive self-image as being unworthy of love and without agency; they also represent others as unpredictable, unresponsive, and untrustworthy. These infants build up very negative internal working models in relation to attachment.

It is essential for young children as social beings that they experience relationships that are reliable and sensitive to their needs. Winnicott (1971a) concluded, when children are responsive and expressive in their facial and body movements parents respond and give them the sensitive care that they need. By observing the subtle, shifting patterns of infant's facial and body movements, parents become aware of their infant's cues and provide further experiences to support them (Murray and Andrews, 2000; Gerhardt, 2004).

Question to Consider

What are the critical periods or everyday interactions? Read the following extract and reflect.

Do You Agree with Stern?

Personalities are conceived as being shaped more by their everyday interactions with parents than by isolated dramatic events or major developmental stages, according to Stern (1985). In contrast to some of the more established sequential stages in behavioural science, Stern asserts there are no critical phases in a child's life, as Freud suggests, within the oral and anal periods of psychoanalysis, but rather a long continuum of smaller but important moments. For him, the infant discovers the first suggestions of autonomy from small acts of assertion. At four months of age the infant may avert their eyes; at about twelve months they have the physical ability to walk away and at eighteen months say, 'No'. All of these are considered acts of will – each infant behaviour influenced by the natural development of the central nervous system. As this evolution continues, self-affirmation creates the sense in an infant's mind that they are an individual with a personalised will.

According to Stern (1985), relationships throughout life continually reshape the inner working model of relationships and therefore an imbalance at one point can be corrected later. Therefore, for Stern there is no crucial period early in life but an on-going, life-long process, with multiple varied emotional connections.

Creating a Cherished Space for Emotional Relationships to Develop

Winnicott's (1960) concept of 'holding', as discussed in previous chapters, complements the notion of 'containment' proposed by Bion, and with the terms are used interchangeably in formal care contexts. This concept has been widened to include the 'holding in mind' of others. The concept of 'containment' (Bion, 1962) describes the process in which the parent/carer is attuned to her infant's state of mind and can hold the infant's uncomfortable feelings in her own mind, which would otherwise threaten to overwhelm the infant. A factor therefore in supporting a carer's capacity for containment is the sufficient external supports from others that perform a similar containing and caring function. However, the concept of containment should also include the carer processing their feelings and thereby transforming them and making them manageable for the infant. This also means taking risks when reflecting on personal experiences that may be challenging, authentically analysing observations, and evaluating practice in formal day care. For practitioners working with children, it can also be about changing established views in the light of new theoretical information or observational evidence. In making practice changes from an emotional perspective, practitioners were able to be more attuned to and self-regulate their own behaviours. One way of developing this is connecting emotions with observations. The Tavistock approach as a way of observing enables the observer to immerse themselves in the interactions that take place between the infant and others present. The observer remains non-interventionist and as unobtrusive as possible, therefore experiencing the everyday interactions. Rustin (2009) in Brooker (2017) defined the intention as 'being present in the moment as fully as possible, open to perceiving as much as possible'. During this observation method, there are no notes, photos, or videos taken by the observer. This is completed after the observation and shared as part of a discussion with colleagues. The focus of the observational discussions includes what was observed but also what was emotionally felt by the observers. Evaluations therefore include the child's behaviour but also capture the atmosphere and whether for example it felt relaxed or tense. The central aspect of the method therefore relies on seeking to understand internal emotional states rather than external factors, leading to a greater contextual insight into children's anxieties and feelings of safety (Elfer, 2006). A study by psychologist Richard Passman (1987) found that children who had a TO had a lower heart rate and lower blood pressure when they were in situations that were mildly stressful, and around 60 per cent of children under three in the study had a TO. The TO supported the children to make the emotional transition from dependence to independence. Transitional objects are a way for very young children to cope with their external world, with Goddard (2016) revealing the lifelong implications of TO in a study of end of life care. TO support children's (and in some cases as they move into adulthood) well-being. Without such an object, true feelings may be concealed, suppressed, or dismissed as the child struggles to cope with their everyday experiences.

Transitional Objects and Transitions

Voice Vignette: Personalised Charts

In formal day care we would have a chart with a photograph of each of the children's cuddles from home. They were clearly labelled and are a source of support when the child needed them. Occasionally they were assigned as a restful sleep comfort and as a group we reflected on and discussed this. We talked about the times of day and when we thought a child should be able to have their comfort toy. We decided as a group it should come from the child, not us, and that they shouldn't be out of reach or hidden. The objects shouldn't need to be only brought out at special times when we felt it was the right time to give it to them or a way to calm down the child. Rather, the objects, including the TO, should be navigated by the children much more and they should be the ones who decide when they want to have it or put it aside as they played. Often the older children would use their objects within and as part of their play. They would either give the object a persona, similar to a peer, or they would create a narrative in their play and the object would be part of that narrative.

Voice Vignette: Transitioning to Sleep in Formal Day Care

Caz jumps on her toy, a big soft dog, as she tries to settle herself to sleep. She wriggles on it and finds comfort in lying on it. The transition to sleep within the nursery seems to be accompanied by some anxiety. Perhaps the routine of sleep time seemed different from her experiences at home. She is two years old and one of a group of eight children. Settling down to sleep with one practitioner she sits and takes off her socks and places them in a plastic basket. She then moves onto the sleep mat near the basket and observes the other children doing the same. She watches for a few seconds before being asked to lie down and settle, and it is at this point that she wriggles on her dog, squirming and moving as she slowly attempts to settle herself to sleep.

It is the transitional space (intermediate area, third area) that is the space of experiencing, between the inner and outer worlds, and contributed by both, in which primary creativity (illusion) exists and can develop ('Transitional Objects and Transitional Phenomena', Winnicott, 1951; further developed in Winnicott, 1971b). From as early as 1945, Winnicott, from within his own concepts of object-relations, approached the infant's developing capacity to discover and adapt to reality. He described first the common patterns of infancy is when a very young baby first finds a thumb, or a fist, to suck, and may stroke their own face, gather a piece of material and suck or stroke it, in this case a cuddly dog, or make babbling noises. Winnicott assumed accompanying fantasy and used the term transitional for these phenomena.

The Symbolic Value of the Transitional Object as Opposed to a Cuddly Toy from Home When Transitioning to Different Spaces and Places

Examples of Transitional Objects and Objects of Attachment: Iggle Piggle

A toy named Iggle Piggle, from a favourite children's television programme, can be a TO. The Iggle Piggle was a TO for a child at a setting and was often brought in when they were late arriving. The child's home life was quite chaotic, and the child seemed to be attached to the toy, talking about the programme associated with it. It was a 15-minute programme which had a calming ambience about it, with stories and songs repeated, and was intended to be watched at bedtime. I wondered if the calming effect and repetition of the programme was as much about the attachment to the object as well as the object itself. The toy was a nursery toy rather than a home toy as well, and the staff had said it was fine for the child to keep it because it had been left behind after another child had started school.

- The infant assumes their rights over the object.
- The object is affectionately cuddled as well as excitedly loved and mutilated.
- It must never change, unless changed by the infant.
- It must service instinctual loving and also hating.
- It must be seen to the infant to give warmth, or to move, or to have texture, or to do something that seems to show it has vitality or reality of its own.
- Inner and outer experiences gained from the TO.

- The transitional object ... is not forgotten and it is not mourned. It loses meaning, and this is because the transitional phenomena have become diffused, have become spread out over the whole intermediate territory between inner psychic reality and the external world (Winnicott, 1971a: 5).

Examples of Transitional Objects and Objects of Attachment: A Ball

Sometimes we assume a TO is soft and cuddly but often they are not and they can come in many forms. A ball for example can be a TO.

Friedrich Froebel was a 19th-century German pedagogue, who was a pioneer in education for very young children. For Froebel a sphere is often a first or favourite toy of infants. It is lightweight and easy to grasp or hold. For Froebel, the sphere symbolized unity because it is a complete whole, a pure form. The whole is the beginning of understanding and everything else is derived from the whole.

Psychotherapy and Transitional Objects

For 50 years, child and adolescent psychotherapist, Monica Lanyado, has focused on how to best treat traumatised children. Her 1985 paper, 'Surviving Trauma', was the beginning of publications about trauma. She began working with children who had been taken into care by social services and her working life has since been devoted to working with fostered and adopted children, either as a clinician or supervising psychotherapists. She trained at the Tavistock Clinic. After her training, which primarily focused on the theories of Melanie Klein, she began to forge her own theoretical pathway, drawing on a diverse range of psychoanalytical thinkers. She set up a new child psychotherapy training at the Scottish Institute of Human Relations.

In developing an understanding about TO as a child transitions from their carer and environment, I have chosen to use Monica Lanyado's example from her MINDinMIND interview (2021) as it provides a description of the complexities and value of TO. It provides an opportunity to reflect on how TO is symbolised and the inner world of the child she supported therapeutically.

Extract Transcription of Lanyado Interview

In a MINDinMIND Interview (2021: 10:25–13:01), Monica Lanyado discussed a ball that was a TO. It was with a four-year-old child she was working with, who was transitioning from his foster parents to adoptive parents, also knowing he had birth parents.

... With this green ball he sort of suddenly became so attached to, in the midst of all this growing tension, which was not spoken about directly to him, but he must have sensed in all the adults around him.

He suddenly attached himself to this ball in a way that was quite new and felt he had to take that ball home with him, and whilst there were lots of battles of control this was entirely different. I could immediately sense that and I went with it.

... so I thought let's see what happens and the fact that this ball became so important to him going in between the session and then home and then he would bring it back to the next session. The in-between of that ball and the fact that he also spent a lot of time sitting on the stairs.

... at that point he was absolutely in-between ... such a no man's land, such a desperate place and yet this ball sustained him. It belonged to both of us, but it didn't really just belong to either of us. It was like a teddy.

... like a teddy that helped to link these two different places. At that point between therapy and his foster home but later on ... between his foster home and his adoptive home.

I said he could take the ball as long as you bring it back, thinking will he bring it back? maybe not at all, but when he did bring it back, the fact that this ball then moved between us and helped to sustain him. He also started to play in ways he hadn't played before which I found extra-ordinary and there was something developmentally which was spurred by these actions. He was held firmly by a very good social worker, a loving foster home and the therapy in trying to explore these deeper issues. He was in a way carried across this very treacherous sort of place in his life where he was very frightened of what was going to happen and at the same time longing for some sort of security. He was also very hurt and rejected that he couldn't stay with his foster family and couldn't under-stand what had happened to his birth family either.

He is only four years old .... the strengths were there if they were given a chance to flourish so I learned an enormous amount from him.

This example gave an insight into the ball that was the TO, moving from place to place but also the emotional holding discussed. I was also interested in the TO being the ball (sphere) as a Froebelian, and although Froebel was embedded in education, his philosophy about children's play links to some of the narrative that Lanyado was reflecting on with her client, the boy and his ball.

The shape of the sphere for Froebel has a special spiritual significance because it is a shape that freely allows the child to experiment with movement in space. According to Flannery Quinn (2013), in her evaluations on *The Education of Man* (*c.*1826) Froebel discussed the ball, as a sphere, which he believes to be the original/universal shape. He explained that the sphere can be used to understand 'energy', which goes forth in all directions equally (Froebel, *c.*1826: 103). It is as an object of play that 'constantly enters into fresh relations with the child', inspiring the earliest forms of discovery and imagination (Froebel, c.1826: 174). The relationship aspects connect to the relationships the boy was encountering, with his ball being his constant.

Leaving the Primary Carer

A growing number of children in the Western world routinely attend organised group-based child care, and thus spend much of their day under non-maternal supervision and care. There is an ongoing debate regarding the implications of this shift from in-home to out-of-the-home care early in children's lives (Belsky and Rovine, 1988), though it seems clear that non-maternal care indeed plays a role in children's development. For example, high quality child care has been linked with enhanced cognitive and academic functioning (Caspi, 2000; NICHD, 2004). Child care quantity, such as the hours spent in day care has been shown to relate to behaviours such as aggression, non-compliance, and other externalising problems. Several studies also find early and extensive child care to be related to increased risk for insecurity of young children's attachment to their mothers. During the transition both infant and parent can feel unsettled and emotional. However, if a healthy attachment between the infant and the family has been nurtured and established, infants can be resilient to the separation, capable of building loving and trusting relationships with other carers, including practitioners, when the relationship has been established (Elfer, Goldschmeid and Sellek, 2011).

Transitions in Formal Day Care

In *The Emotional Life of the Toddler*, Alicia Lieberman (2018: 282) discusses how spending the day in formal day care, the act of saying goodbye is the most noticeable aspect of the parents' departure but it marks only the beginning of the separation process. The child is now faced with a long day away from the parent. The being apart arouses all sorts of feelings of anxiety and stress with a reliance on coping resources. However, there are ways of keeping the parent's reassuring image alive in the heart and mind of the child. There are development differences in the ease with which the child can adapt to being away from the primary parent. Between 12 and 18 months there is an increase in the child's distress over separation, and Lieberman evaluates in her work that after 20–24 months most children have an easier time being away from their parent. Lieberman reports this becomes more pronounced after the second year when toddlers' sustained progress in areas of memory, language, and symbolic play means that they can bring more sophisticated cognitive and emotional skills to that task. Therefore, there is an argument that, for the child, the later they begin formal day care, the more likely that the child will adjust to it smoothly. Full-time child care can also be more burdensome to the child attending than shorter daily separations and part-time child care puts less strain on the child's resources than a full ten hours away from home. It also highlights the importance that settings should offer the child familiar and reassuring reminders of their parent's presence, so the child's external life together bridges and reduces the anxiety.

Agency of Voice: Ways of Listening to Children in Supporting Transitions

Parents dropping in to the setting during lunchtime or making a phone call is particularly useful with babies and toddlers can be helpful to provide a sense of continuity even if the baby or child is non-verbal. They can recognise their parent's voice and cherish that connection, although often there is more anxiety from the adults that this contact will cause more distress. Although it may disrupt the child's care routine, a phone call for a talk acknowledges the child is important in their family's life and provides a familiar voice for the child as they experience different spaces and places.

Listening to children's voices is frequently discussed in early years work but what does it really mean? Much of what is written is to guide practitioners in their work of listening to children. The United Nations Convention on the Rights of the Child (UNCRC), especially article 12, outlines that children should be allowed to participate and be consulted in matters that affect them. Many nation states have embedded the articles of the UNCRC within legislation; the emphasis is on shared responsibility to uphold the articles, particularly on issues of voice affecting children in their home and within professional contacts. Listening to the views of children within early years settings promotes practices that encourage practitioners to share time and space with the children in their care and become attuned to their needs (Henderson, 2018: 23).

In Scotland, a new infant pledge (Scottish Government, 2023) has been issued, outlining best practice on how to take account of infants' views and rights. It recognises the child's needs and is proposed as a way England could follow similar guidance, recognising the child's needs are part of the family and child care relationship. New guidelines on how to take account of infants' views and rights in all encounters with professionals in statutory or third sector services, or in public spaces, have been published by the Scottish Government. 'The voice of the infant: Best practice guidelines and infant pledge' (Scottish Government, 2023) is co-produced by a short-life working group, on behalf of the Infant Mental Health Implementation and Advisory Group, part of the Scottish Government's Perinatal and Infant Mental Health Programme Board. The infant pledge sets out what infants should expect from those around them. The Scottish Government said the pledge 'encourages mindful commitment to facilitate infants to express their feelings, and to consider their views, uphold their rights and take action accordingly', and it is 'a reminder it is everyone's responsibility to listen to the voice of infants'. The guidance is primarily written for all those who meet and work with babies and very young children through their work in community settings and nurseries, and in education, third sector, health, and social services, both general and specialist (Oxtoby, 2023).

The guidance offers suggestions about how those who work with babies and very young children can notice, facilitate, and share the infant's feelings, ideas, and preferences that they communicate to us through their gaze, body language, and vocalisations. As well as physical space, emotional space is needed to properly take account of the baby's perspective. Emotions felt by those accompanying the baby will be communicated to them and may stop the baby from feeling at ease, and being receptive to attempts to engage them. In therapeutic encounters, it is important to try to attend to everyone's feelings and help create this emotional space. During home visits, it may be necessary to address these important issues with the parents. This voice of the child is heard and seen in the noises and movements they make, their response to the environment, and in their interactions with the people who are with them. Their silence may also represent a communication and it is important to understand this in the context of their history and relationships. It assumes that all children and young people have views and opinions about their own health care and actively encourages them to express what matters to them (Scottish Government, 2023). It is often helpful for professionals and caregivers to adopt an approach of shared curiosity to infant communication. Describing aloud what the infant is doing, wondering together about what it means, and being open to different interpretations is supportive of infant expression, provides feedback to the infant, and offers insights to both caregivers and professionals.

This also includes observations and what non-human objects the child engages with:

- Do they have a TO?
- When does the TO appear to be wanted, forgotten?
- How does the child communicate with their TO?

As with eliciting voice, this requires careful consideration of the context as well as the method of communication with babies and very young children.

The Practitioner as a Professional: The Key Person in Formal Day Care

In England, formal day care, which includes home-based childminders, creches, family centres, home and purpose-built day nursery settings, is regulated by the education authority, following an Early Years Foundation Stage curriculum (DfE, 2021). Practitioners working in these contexts are expected to be appropriately qualified and deemed suitable regarding health and safety and safeguarding risks. The practitioner, as a key person, generally has responsibilities for a small group of infants, with a vested interest, promoting an intimate relationship with each of the individual infants within the group, supporting their development, and acting as the key point of contact with the infant's parents (DfE, 2021).

Key aspects of a key person relationship: *Stop*, *Look*, and *Listen*.

- Be available.
- Be tuned in.
- Be responsive.
- Be consistent.

Listening to the Child and the Shifting Value of the Transitional Object

Voice Vignette 1: The Silky Scarf

At lunch time, Sue, a mother who works down the road, comes and breast-feeds her baby three times a week. Occasionally, dad comes too and will help change the nappy or chat to his partner. When this was first discussed at the induction session, I was quite anxious how it was going to work with the other babies in the setting and quite frankly was a little put off with the inconvenience! The baby was 11 months old, and I wasn't sure how long she was going to continue to breastfeed her. I had assumed for a few months, but soon realised she wanted to continue indefinitely.

We created a space for her in the nursery and, as the weeks followed, a pattern soon emerged and I was surprised how smoothly it went. She priori-tised her time with her baby and when she left he would snuggle into his smelly silk scarf and fall asleep, content. He didn't carry the scarf all day but when he became tired or tearful, he would call for it and snuggle up to it and chew it, twisting it around his finger. I felt the silk scarf reduced some of his anxiety and he became aware of the lunch time pattern too. It worked well but made me acutely aware of the other infants I cared for (we had five others in the room) and their observations. In a way, I felt protective of them …

Voice Vignette 2: A Favourite Teddy

Bev, a mother, has reluctantly decided to send her baby Amy to nursery as she has to return to work but is not quite emotionally ready and wants to con-tinue breastfeeding Amy for longer than she had initially anticipated. She is angry and offensive towards the nursery staff as they try to settle Amy in and Amy herself seems unsettled and anxious. Amy is 10 months old. At the end of the trial morning the baby room supervisor sits down with Bev and allows her to talk about her feelings returning to work and sending Amy to the nursery. She is accepting of the situation as she verbalises her reasons, although it is very clear, emotionally, that Bev is resisting the change. The room supervisor asks Bev how she feels and what they can do to support her. Bev cries and states she feels overwhelmed and a failure at parenting. Together they plan and reflect on what could work for Bev and Amy. They create and think about sharing practices and how they could bring home into the setting more. They encourage Bev to bring in cuddle blankets from home that smell of her so Amy can snuggle up and smell them to help settle her. Amy also has a favourite teddy, and Bev is encouraged to bring this in, so the teddy can be used and navigated by Amy rather than the adults around her. As the two connect and communicate together, both begin to feel calmer and more supported. Amy is cared for by one special key person at the setting who also spends time with Bev daily.

Voice Vignette 3: Peter the Rabbit

Jake had a little stuffed rabbit toy called Peter who slept with him day and night. Peter was part of Jake's family and accompanied him to nursery on his first day. Knowing that Peter was going to be with him provided comfort and security in the transition process from the familiar to the unfamiliar. He was allowed to keep it keep it close and during the first few weeks it provided a connection to home, which made being away from it bearable. Such specific attachment items are known as Transitional Objects. The object allowed Jake to have some consistency and predictability in unknown situations.

Voice Vignette 4: Muffy the Toy

Muffy had a chair at the family dining table, a pillow to sit against on the couch, and a place in my son's arms at every social gathering – held, hugged, clutched, and carried. Muffy was an instrumental part of my son's daily life, and upon my son's start of school, Muffy remained at home and 'waited' for my son to return. Upon my son's return, he and Muffy reunited daily in fierceness and fortitude, joy and happiness, and relief in the reunion. Until that one day when Muffy was not immediately retrieved or sought after, as my son had brought a friend home from school. Instead, Muffy was relegated to limbo, sitting on the threshold (both literally and metaphorically) until my son's friend departed. After this social visit, Muffy became permanently positioned on the periphery, as further encounters between my son and his friends would ensue. Sometimes my son's friends would bring their own special toys from home, those objects that were meaningful to them, and Muffy would resurface. These objects, like Muffy, were held, hugged, and hoisted in the air until finally one day they were ignored (Goddard, 2018: 3).

In these examples, the TO had become the emotional stabilizer as well as a social connector. The TO was an of attachment that was used to support social relatedness and evoke empathy as the child connected with the objects of others in very deep and meaningful ways. These objects are both representational of home and relational in terms of the role they play in social engagements, school experiences, and throughout the course of a child's overall development (Brenner, 2004, in Goddard, 2016).

The TO is a 'relationship object', and is part of a 'relational way of being'.

Questions to Consider

- Do you notice the TO that children bring in? Do you tune into these?
- What are the children trying to communicate about their TO?
- Are the children saying 'Look at me! Notice me!'

Scenting Transitional Objects: The Power of Smells

Transitional Objects are most effective when they are made from natural absorbent materials that take on scents well. The cotton and bamboo Cuski comforters are designed with this in mind. Cuski comforters are all flat bodied and made with cotton (Figure 5.2) (Littlejohns, 2022).

This is making a TO smell like the parent, which can sound a little unsavoury but is calming to the child. The smell evokes feeling safe and being able to smell the parent indicates they are near. Young children are reliant on their senses and smell is a hugely powerful sense. A scented TO enables them

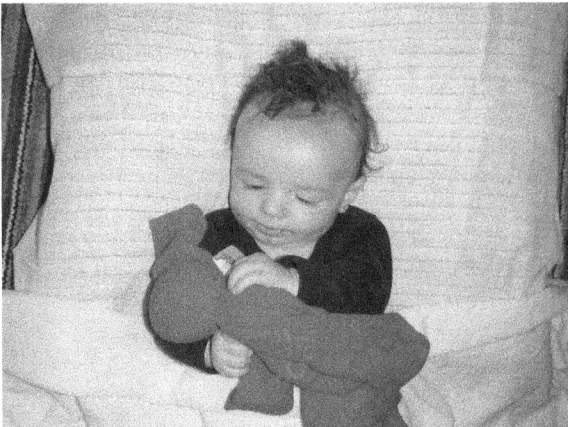

Figure 5.2 A 'Cuski' TO has been given to an infant as a gift. He began to rely on it and would often suck it and hold it close when he went to sleep or was taken to a new place or new adult. The head was ball shaped and is another reminder of the sphere, the ball, as discussed by Frobel earlier in this chapter.

to support bonding with this object. Combining a TO with other calming cues offers babies and children a safe and calming environment that is soothing and reassuring, especially as they settle into new places and spaces with and without their parent.

Settling into Formal Day Care

Settling into formal day care for a child, irrespective of their age, can be a challenging and emotional period for both the parent and the child and requires a period of adjustment. As they gradually realise that their parent is separate to them this can cause frustration and anxiety. In this stressful period their special toy, a TO, can help. It represents the safety and loving parental relationship. Basically, it provides reassurance until the real deal, that's you, arrives.

Voice Vignette

As a parent, I remember wanting the settling-in phase to be done with yesterday. As an educator, I get asked the same question every year, 'How long will my child take to settle in?' I wish the answer was as simple as the question. Each child is unique and takes their own time. We can only help with the transition phase by easing their separation anxiety and comforting the child.

It can be very beneficial to introduce a comfort object while settling in children to nursery and school, and in other situations (Valrani, 2023). Therefore, TO often help during transitions. This can be the transition between sleep cycles when babies often stir, but the comfort of the object can mean they avoid waking fully. Children often find they help with the transition of going into nursery or other care settings without you. They help them to feel safe and are therefore calmer and less likely to be upset. As they develop a stronger attachment to the TO, it can help them feel safer and offer more reassurance.

In formal day care, it is important that practitioners understand how important TO are to some children. They

- Are a healthy part of child development.
- Are a valuable and common part of child development.
- Can potentially cause children stress and anxiety, if taken away from them.
- Are not a sign of weak or insecure children.
- Need to be considered in your setting to help ease separation anxiety.

Some advice that practitioners can give parents about bringing special TO to the nursery include:

- Inviting the child to choose one 'special' TO to bring to nursery/school rather than several.

- Having a special place/container where TO can be placed so that children can still see them and know they are still there.
- Having two or more duplicate versions of the TO, if possible, in the eventuality that one gets lost or has to be washed.
- Bringing in a special bag where children know they can put their TO.
- Not using a TO as a bribe or taking it away as a punishment as this can cause anxiety.
- Having a TO that is easy for the child to carry around.
- Not placing a time frame when a child's TO should be taken away, when children are ready, their need for their much loved and treasured object will lessen (Lorelli, 2022).

Transitional Objects and Early Years Policies: Holistic Focus on the Flourishing and Well-Being of the Child

The 'eudaemonic', that is, achieving individual happiness and well-being through an ethical educational approach, is a process conducive to achievement which allows children to flourish. It is needed now because of the negative impacts of global crises on children and childhood. These include:

- The pandemic.
- Poverty.
- Health and mental well-being.
- Population movement through war and climate breakdown.
- Changing and diverse family structures.
- Digital childhoods and growth of artificial intelligence.

The realisation of human potential through the 'eudaemonic' needs a greater spotlight to how we evidence children beyond an outcomes-based approach within research. Data often tell 'what', but little about the 'how'. Supporting well-being and flourishing childhoods, although gaining momentum, remains relatively understudied within early years. This includes:

- Authentically listening to children.
- Slowing down.
- Accepting the child as they are and where they are starting.
- Our positions, beliefs, and attitudes.
- Having an ethical approach and allowing children to flourish.
- Ways to evidence.

The need for tentative research designs acknowledges the role of context and the focus on the real world. It is concerned with the daily life in the setting as it happens. By providing a more detailed and nuanced focus on the interaction and relatedness between context processes and outcomes, they are conceptualised from other theoretical points of view. This raises questions about how practice is related with children's well-being involvement and learning, which are inclusive and collaborative. In exploring TOs and their conceptual and practical knowledge within settings, a broad overview of how the policies include them is explored. Some settings seem to have embedded the understanding about well-being and TO, whilst other policies insinuate the TO as being beneficial in the short term but ultimately guided by the adults and their perspective of the use of them rather than by the child themselves.

Formal Day Care Setting Policies about Transitions and TO: Examples from Policy to Practice

In formal day care, transitions are experienced over and over. A parent says goodbye and the child responds in a cathartic release of emotion. It is in these moments where the healing power of TO is fully utilised. A parent may offer their child an old t-shirt they have worn and the sensorial elements calm and support the child through the good-bye, as they metaphorically and physically hold on to the promise of their return. As an early childhood educator, prior to the start of school, I visited every family in their home and asked parents what their child's TO was. Most families shared that their child was fine and did not have or need anything. Once school began, however, it was observed that the same children often used self-chosen objects that they had discovered in the classroom and at home, such as a scarf left unintentionally, as a security blanket (Hagan, 2014).

One setting described the importance of TO as part of their policy. This included how they described the object as a reminder or comforter in times of separation. Taking the child's object away can cause distress and upset, so the use and availability of TO is encouraged and supported, as well as providing the security of a practitioner.

The settings outlined ideas to help children play but still feel comforted:

1   Children could bring special bags in to put their objects in.
2   They could have a box in the room where they could put their objects, so they are still in sight.
3   The number of TO should be reduced, with one 'special' one that is easily transported.

The expectation for children in early years is therefore that the TO should be placed into something visible, but not something they would encourage children to hold. They also outlined that when a child enters pre-school (at three years old), room discussions with parents and the child will take place and the key person will plan visits. The existing key person and the child's new key person will both spend time with the child in the new learning environment. Transition in this sense therefore is concerned with the change a child encounters from one place to another. As children develop from birth throughout childhood they move, or transition, from one learning environment or setting to a new one. Often, these transitions involve a process of change that requires them to adapt their thoughts, feelings, and behaviours to meet new expectations. By the time a child reaches school age they may have already experienced several transition periods, including:

- The transition from home to the setting.
- The transition between room bases.
- The transition from one provider to another during the working week.
- The transition from a child care provider to a school.

Transition, like a journey, takes time, preparation, and planning. Adults can help a child's journey into new territory by supporting them before, during, and after the transition occurs. Parents and practitioners work together, and the children should feel as comfortable, confident, and emotionally secure as possible when entering the early years setting. Young children starting a nursery need support to enable them to adjust to a temporary separation from their family. They need to feel that they are a valuable, competent member of the new social group and they need to develop positive attitudes towards the range of new experiences they will encounter. During the transition children need to be helped to retain the self-confidence and self-respect that they have already gained at home or in previous settings. It is accepted that TO are brought into the formal day care setting, but the child is encouraged to place them and keep them on their peg (day nursery carer, anon, 2023).

Another setting recognised transitions as being a multi-layered approach although TO were not mentioned in the policy.

- We believe that all our children and their families deserve support at points of transition.
- We recognise that periods of transition include major changes such as first entry to our setting and the move to a new setting or into school. We also know that children need support to change rooms or key person and also with day-to-day transitions such as being welcomed into our setting each morning and helped to share their experiences with parents when it is time to go home.
- We know that we have a statutory duty within the curriculum to provide each child with a key person who should help them to become familiar with our setting and to feel confident and safe within it, developing a genuine bond with the child and family and offering a settled, close relationship.
- We also have a statutory responsibility to share relevant information about a child with parents and other settings that they may attend.
- We recognise that more vulnerable children and families may need additional support at points of transition.

Voice Vignette: A Dialogue

In discussion with practitioners from a different child care setting (within a national nursery chain) the similarities in discourses are prevalent. They were asked about Transitional Objects and their thoughts about them. They agreed they were important as cuddle toys and a reminder from home. They did not seem to have extensive knowledge about the psychological background regarding TO, although they knew they were a comfort when transitioning. They also agreed that the lead practitioner would not encourage the children to walk around with them or have them once they were in the pre-school room. They gave examples of a large toy being dragged around and the difference between bringing in numerous toys and if these were in fact temporary comfort toys rather than symbolically important TO.

Another setting outlined transitions involving a process of change that required a period of adjustment for the family and their child. Information is shared (learning journey) and is the child's starting point. They included policies about:

- Settling in procedures.
- Role of key person.
- Comforters/objects of reference.
- Parents pack/outline of routine/policies.

In keeping with attachment theory and the need for children to build secure relationships, the national guidelines insist that each child must be assigned a key person.

> Providers must inform parents and/or carers of the name of the key person, and explain their role, when a child starts attending a setting. The key person must help ensure that every child's learning and care is tailored to meet their individual needs. The key person must seek to engage and support parents and/or carers in guiding their child's development at home. At times of transition (such as shift changes), make sure staff greet and say goodbye to babies and their key person. This helps to develop secure and trusting three-way relationships. Some children might like to keep a favourite or cuddly toy with them to begin with as a TO although little else is mentioned about the object.
>
> (PACEY, 2014)

Another setting in their documentation outlined what should/can my child bring to the nursery and states that toys or other objects from the family home should not be brought into the nursery. Many settings in England followed guidance from the Department for Education (DfE, 2021) and have retained the policy. It includes that comforters are an important TO to help support children's emotional security during unsettling times.

Voice Vignette: The Advice from Settings Was Often Included in the Following Narrative

If you notice that your young child is starting to become attached to a security object, you may want to buy another so you can switch them when one needs washing. But don't wait too long or the new one won't have the feel of the original one. There is no best age to phase these out, but some parents feel that the transition from toddler to pre-school (around age three) might be a good time. When phasing out transition objects, use a gradual approach: 'Let's put your blanket over on the shelf for ten minutes while we play'. Gradually increase the time that the security blanket is out of easy reach. Be supportive and talk about what you are doing. Try saying,

> I see that you don't have your stuffed lamb with you all the time. When you go to preschool, we are going to try leaving your lamb at home. Today, let's try leaving it at home while we go to the playground. We don't want your lamb to get dirty.
>
> (Bright Horizons, 2023, n.p.)

During 2020, dummies and hard surface toys were encouraged to be sterilised on arrival at the setting and before returning home. Blankets and soft toys had to remain in the child's bag throughout the day and were given to children at sleep times and at times during the day when needed. If children needed their comforter during the day outside of sleep times they would be given to children for a period and then removed when the practitioner felt they were able to support children through positive interactions. Parents also had to duplicate comforters to keep at the setting and these also had to be washed daily. This became part of the daily routine and for many children the use of a TO was actively discouraged and certainly washing the object regularly was encouraged.

This was a significant shift to how TO were perceived in early years settings and the next chapter outlines the move to them as being quite threatening during the pandemic. It shows, with examples of how settings have created opportunities for a revival, the value in recognising the eudaemonic aspect of them, achieving individual happiness and well-being through an ethical educational approach, a process conducive to achievement, which allows children to flourish.

A Final Note

This chapter has aimed to bridge the theory around TO and the practicality of it being helpful as part of formal day care transitional policies. It has included ways that TO could be included and consolidates the importance and theory to the value of children's self-selected objects as they move from space, place, and people significant in their lives. Vignettes have been included to provide some rich examples of practice as a way of giving meaning to the value of TO.

References

Barnes, P. (1995) *Personal, Social and Emotional Development of Children*. Milton Keynes: Blackwell Publishing.

Belsky, J. and Rovine, M. (1988) Nonmaternal care in the first year of life and the security of infant attachment. *Child Development*, 59: 157–167.

Belsky, J., Burchinal, M., McCartney, K., Vandell, D., Clarke-Stewart, K., and Owen, M. T. (2007). Are there long term effects of early child care? *Child Development*, 78 (2): 681–701.

Bion, W. R. (1962). *Learning from Experience*. London: Heinemann.

Booth, A. and Dunn, J. F., eds. (1994). *Stepfamilies: Who Benefits? Who Does Not?* Hillsdale, NJ: Lawrence Erlbaum.

Bowlby, J. (1969) *Attachment and loss, Vol. I: Attachment*. New York: Basic Books.

Bowlby, J. (2005) *The Making and Breaking of Affectionate Bonds*. London: Routledge.

Brenner, M. (2004) *The Complete Guide to Transitional Objects*. New York: Simon & Schuster.

Bright Horizons (2023) How to smooth transitions and change routines. Available at: brighthorizons.co.uk (accessed October 14, 2023).

Brooker, K. (2017) Observing to understand – using the Tavistock method of observation to support reflective practice. British Educational Research Association. July 19. Available at: www.bera.ac.uk/blog/observing-to-understand-using-the-tavistock-method-of-observation-to-support-reflective-practice

Caspi, A. (2000) The child is father of the man: Personality continuities from childhood to adulthood. *Journal of Personality and Social Psychology*, 8(1): 158–172. https://doi.org/10.1037//0022-3514.78.1.158

Cooper, T. and Roth, I. (2003) *Challenging Psychological Issues*. Milton Keynes: Open University Press.

Department for Education (2021) *The Revised Early Years Foundation Stage*. London: Department for Education. Available at: www.gov.uk/government/publications/early-years-foundation-stage-framework–2

Elfer, P. (2006) Exploring children's expressions of attachment in nursery. *European Early Childhood Education Journal*, 14 (2): 81–96.

Elfer, P., Goldschmied, E., and Selleck, D. (2011) *Key Persons in the Nursery Building Relationships for Quality Provision*. London: David Fulton Books.

Flannery Quinn, S. (2013) Frobels Gifts. Available at: www.eymatters.co.uk/wp-content/uploads/2020/05/Froebels-Gifts.pdf (accessed June 30, 2023).

Froebel, F. (*c.*1826, trans. 1912). *Froebel's Chief Writings on Education*, trans. S. S. F. Fletcher and J. Welton. London: Edward Arnold.

Gerhardt, S. (2004) *Why Love Matters*. London: Routledge.

Goddard, C. (2016) The sacred language of objects: How end-of-life doulas experience the use of transitional objects as a significant part of the dying process. Fielding

Graduate University ProQuest Dissertations Publishing, 10100532. Available at: www.proquest.com/openview/0dee5c618d4d553f983a9fbb34512ddd/1?pq-origsite= gscholar&cbl=18750

Goddard, C. (2018) The significance of transitional objects in an early childhood classroom for children and teachers. *Dimensions of Early Childhood*, 46 (1): 6–9. Available at: https://static1.squarespace.com/static/55972ad4e4b02838d12b67fd/t/ 5b92b64e2b6a2848d3a901a8/1536341597887/Importance+of+Transitional+Objects. +C.+Goddard.pdf

Hagan, E. (2014) More than just teddy bears: Transitional objects allow a child's inherent sense of self to emerge. *Psychology Today*, July 15, 2014. Available at: www. psychologytoday.com/gb/blog/the-guest-room/201407/more-just-teddy-bears (accessed October 2, 2023).

Henderson, E. (2018) *Autoethnography in Early Childhood and Educational Care*. London: Routledge.

Lanyado, M. (1985) Surviving trauma: Dilemmas in the psychotherapy of traumatised children. *British Journal of Psychotherapy*, 2 (1): 50–62.

Lanyado, M. (2021) Interview with Monica Lanyado. *Mind in Mind*, February 19. Available at: https://mindinmind.org.uk/interviews/monica-lanyado-interview/ (accessed October 2, 2023).

Lieberman, A. (2018) *The Emotional Life of the Toddler*. London: Simon & Schuster.

Littlejohns, R. (2022) Transitional objects: Why that special toy matters. *Calm Family*, January 17. Available at: https://calmfamily.org/transitional-objects-why-that-specia l-toy-matters/ (accessed October 2, 2023).

Lorelli, M. (2022) How transitional objects can help young children with separation anxiety in early years. *Twinkl*, October 11. Available at: www.twinkl.co.uk/news/ how-transitional-objects-can-help-young-children-with-separation-anxiety-in-early-yea rs#:~:text=Dolls%2C%20soft%20toys%20or%20blankets,alternative%20but%20equa lly%20important%20ones (accessed October 2, 2023).

Murray, L. and Andrews, L. (2000) *The Social Infant: Understanding Babies' Communication from Birth*. Richmond: CP Publishing.

NICHD Early Child Care Research Network (2004) Are child developmental outcomes related to before- and after-school care arrangements? Results from the NICHD study of early childcare. *Child Development*, 75 (1): 280–295.

Oxtoby, K. (2023) Scotland: New infant pledge published by government. *Early Years Educator*, March 31. Available at: https://www.earlyyearseducator.co.uk/news/article/ scotland-new-infant-pledge-published-by-government (accessed October 2, 2023).

PACEY (2014) Transitions and settling in: A guide to help you think about how you can support the transitions and settling in processes that the children in your care experience. *Professional Association for Childcare and Early Years*. Available at: www.pacey.org.uk/Pacey/media/Website-files/school%20ready/PG10-transitions-and-settling-in.pdf (accessed October 2, 2023).

Passman, R. H. (1987). Attachments to inanimate objects: Are children who have security blankets insecure? *Journal of Consulting and Clinical Psychology*, 55 (6): 825–830. https://doi.org/10.1037/0022-006X.55.6.825

Scottish Government (2023) Voice of the infant: Best practice guidelines and infant pledge. Available at: www.gov.scot/publications/voice-infant-best-practice-guideline s-infant-pledge/pages/5/ (accessed October 2, 2023).

Stern, D. N. (1985) *The Interpersonal World of the Infant*. New York: Basic Books.

Valrani, M. (2023) The benefits of transitional objects. *Ladybird Nursery*. Available at: https://ladybirdnursery.ae/the-benefits-of-transitional-objects/ (accessed October 2, 2023).

Winnicott, D. W. (1951) *Transitional Objects and Transitional Phenomena*. London: Tavistock.

Winnicott, D. W.(1960/2018) *The Maturational Processes and the Facilitating Environment: Studies in the Theory of Emotional Development*. London: Routledge.

Winnicott, D. W. (1971a) *Playing and Reality*. London: Tavistock.

Winnicott, D. W. (1971b) The use of an object and relating through identifications. In *Playing and Reality*. New York: Basic Books, 86–94.

Chapter 6

Transitional Objects in Early Years and Caring Contexts

This chapter focuses on the way Transitional Objects (TO) have been understood and accepted in formal day care, with reference to young children's emotional, health, and hygiene behaviour, and play, framed around setting policies. Practitioners' perspectives will be examined with their own understanding of the connections to transition objects, attachment, and security. Soft items and some personal objects were discouraged during the pandemic because of the concern about cross-contamination and in order to comply with health and hygiene regulations. Subsequently, parents had to think about creative ways they could continue to support their young child during transitions to formal day care, and this included sewing a patch of their cuddle cloth to their inside jumper sleeve, or sterilising objects more frequently. Day care settings also refused TO, with a misunderstanding or misinformed understanding about the objects children could bring in, some being a TO and other objects representing something else in the child's thinking. Transitional Objects will therefore be explored in developing and widening the dialogue about their value to those working with young children, the way policy could be developed from the pandemic, as well as ensuring the child remains at the heart of practice.

Transitional Objects and an Overview of Children's Emotions

Formal day care attendance is frequently accessed in England and therefore plays an important role in many children's development. Fortuna et al. (2014) study explored a twin design to estimate relative environmental and genetic contributions to the presence of object attachment and assess whether formal day care settings explain some of the environmental variation in their development. They concluded that children who spent half-days in settings were significantly less likely to attach to objects than children who attended full time. Object attachment can therefore be thought of as constituting a protective factor (Rutter, 1985). Although the object a child's takes to the setting cannot provide reassurance, guidance, or affection, its physical presence is sufficient to provide the child with a sense of protection. Winnicott (1953)

DOI: 10.4324/9781003296669-9

emphasised that the use of TO, whilst not needed by all children, is still considered the norm of, healthy development. The few empirical studies and surveys available on this developmental phenomenon, however, have suggested that attachment to objects is not necessarily universal and more of a Westernised 'need' by children. In Western countries, object attachments were found to be common (Van Ijzendoorn et al., 1983), with rates reaching as high as 60 per cent in populations surveyed (Litt, 1981; Lehman et al., 1992). Nevertheless, in other cultures, particularly those in which young children spend much of their time co-sleeping and in close proximity to their mother (or primary carer), rates were found to be significantly lower (Gaddini and Gaddini, 1970; Litt, 1981). Attachment to inanimate objects has therefore been hypothesised to develop as an adaptation to child-rearing practices, such as amount of physical contact, sleeping arrangements, and the extent to which children need to cope with frequent separations from their mothers. This chapter therefore raises the questions about how TO are perceived and, considering the previous chapter, how much knowledge and emphasis is placed on the TO during settling times and the perspectives of those working in formal day care (Lehman et al., 1992; Fortuna et al., 2014).

Voice Vignette: Sleep and Transitional Object (TO)

Day rest and sleep times should be met as part of the routine rather than as a period of reduced care. In formal day care settings sleep patterns may be established and supported with TO, with the personalised care an extension of the child's care at home. Familiarity of using the same cot or bed and establishing a quiet time, prior to sleep, is helpful in creating a calm and relaxing environment. Many group care settings have recently updated their sleep rooms, describing them as nesting rooms, including soft furnishings and neutral colours to create a restful ambience. Cots have been replaced with floor baskets to enable the infant to be able to crawl in and out and reduce the separation of wake and sleep time. The infant can enter the basket themselves and wake at a level they can again move from. This potentially reduces the anxiety revolving around forcing sleep times with little autonomy from the infant themselves (www.naturesleep.co.uk).

Question to Consider

Does this perhaps reinforce the value of treating sleep time in the same way as play time in day care?

Winnicott (1953, 1958) believed the connection to the Transitional Object (TO) was in bridging the inner world of the infant to the outer world. He saw the TO as initiating a sense of imaginative play and young children gaining a sense of their separateness from the environment they are in and the beginning of a relationship with the outside world. He also considered their use both positively and negatively and did not propose mothers initiate their use and extend the duration of TO in the popular assumption they are desirable and necessary for sound emotional development. Winnicott (1953) theorised that TO help children manage the stress of separation from the mother. Bowlby (1969) described children's treatment of their favoured object as a substitute for their 'natural' attachment figure when the person that is typically relied upon for comfort in anxiety-inducing situations is temporarily unavailable. Some support for this exists, demonstrating that for some children the emotional connection they develop to their comforters appears to reduce anxiety around separation experiences from their caregivers and facilitates smooth separations (Passman, 1977; Winnicott, 1987)). For example, children were observed to use their attachment objects as they separated not just from home to setting but also from professional caregivers during the day spent attending the setting (Triebenbacher and Tegano, 1993). In another study, children who were described by their mothers as independent and to have few difficulties going to bed (a form of separation) had significantly higher rates of object attachment than dependent children and those considered having sleep problems (Boniface and Graham, 1979).

Interestingly the purpose and navigation of the TO in formal day care is often led by the practitioner's own perception and experiences about caring for a child, rather than the child themselves. For Winnicott it was the spontaneity attachment of use and the inner creativity of the child in processing their inner and outer reality. The emphasis therefore would be directed towards reducing anxiety and the permanence of the object during times when external things and familiar people (parents) are 'hiding' or 'gone'. Winnicott makes a clear rationale for reflecting on the individual child and allowing them to take the lead in what sooths them through this process rather than forcing an object upon them (Davis and Wallbridge, 1991).

TO and Children in Formal Day Care

According to the New York University Psychoanalytical Institute, the Transitional Object may be conceived of in three ways:

1   As typifying a phase in a child's development.
2   As a defence against separation anxiety.
3   As a neutral sphere in which experience is not challenged.

In many settings, Transitional Objects find their way from home and are not a challenge to the practitioners. They view the TO as a way for the child to develop self-awareness and meet their self-regulatory needs. TO are personified instruments of self-expression and this is synonymously supported, acknowledged, and honoured by their practitioners (SRCD, 2023).

According to developmental psychologist Robert Kegan, development is not possible without self-referential contexts and meanings. Meanings, according to him, are founded on the features each child makes of the stimuli they engage with. This includes the people around them as well as the object (s) they receive, choose, or discover, which for them have an internal life of their own. The object allows for and invites emotional well-being, and without such an object, true feelings may be concealed, suppressed, or dismissed as the infant/child has no other means by which to cope with, comprehend, and contend with the world.

In settings children may carry pillows or stuffed animals they discover in the classroom. They may hold on to them persistently until the parent returns, and then at other times release these items with utter abandonment. In other situations, parents would often apologise for their child's TO, which would be hidden in purses and backpacks, with a sense of guilt that their child cannot cope or be 'independent' without their comforter. Perhaps this is perceived as a measurement of how well a parent has parented their child? The first 'not me' possession, the self-chosen TO, should not be considered detrimental but provide comfort, solace, and predictability representational of a stable and predictable world (Goddard, 2014).

Fundamental to a child's healthy development in formal day care settings are the stable, positive, and close relationships they have with their practitioner as a key person. Children need to be validated to feel good about themselves with adults around them. If children are not paid attention to and their needs or feelings not listened to, they can feel emotionally rejected by the adults around them. This can potentially and unintentionally happen with practitioners who may not know how to support or meet children's needs emotionally. An ethnographic study in a preschool in Sweden advocated the use of TO; however, at the same time, this institution also implemented very specific ground rules in terms of how, where, and when the object could be used. This particular response gives way to the debatable aspects of the use of TO and the understanding about them, as well as the practitioner's own experiences of having a TO. Why are TO perceived as socially unacceptable, restricted, and allocated to certain times and places? Removing or denying access to them can create more anxiety and discord within the child. Research further indicates that those children who were deprived of object relations were often suggested to be more potentially susceptible to long-term pathological disorders. In addition, the usage, availability, and consideration of such objects can enhance the connectedness between child and adult and amongst children themselves (Goddard, 2014).

Another consideration is that early years practitioners, along with others in the 'helping' professions, may have an image of themselves as giving, caring people with an 'ambition to love and be of service to humanity', who may therefore be looking to the children to 'fit the contours of their own ambitions' (Selleck and Griffin, 1996 cited in Dahlberg, Moss, and Pence, 1999). A practitioner may have decided to enter the profession of caring for infants because of their own childhood experiences or the way they were parented. If a child responds according to what the practitioner is conveying, then this can in part work successfully with the development of making emotional connections with each other. However, for many children in formal day care settings, their behaviour can also be perceived as challenging at times, and they can also reject practitioners' approaches to caring for them and resist the façade presented to them if the emotional connection is lacking. Parents may also feel anxious, and challenge and criticise the practices and care. Bain and Barnett (1986) suggested, if the predominant motivation to work with infants arises from unresolved childhood experiences, practitioners may then feel angry and resentful when their own needs are not being met within the child–practitioner relationship. This can lead practitioners to blame infants' behaviours, parents, managers, or co-workers and may develop into a complicated process of transference and projection. Whilst psychotherapists have a specialised and in-depth knowledge about these areas in their clinical practices, many practitioners working in formal day care receive a generalised and often quite limited training and support in understanding about therapeutic relationships when working with children. Many courses attended by practitioners also rely on the educational value and regulations informed by a national curriculum, with less attention given to exploration of the complexities of 'caring' as a profession and the psychological aspects of working with young children and their families.

It is essential, therefore, that practitioners are able gain the maturity and a sense of self-awareness to fulfil their role as a key person through supervision and further continuous professional development. They should be able to have the training and opportunities to look at and reflect on their own motivations and understand where they come from, and through the knowledge they gain about themselves, to better understand and adjust their responses to the infants in their care (Goleman, 1995; Manning-Morton and Thorpe, 2003).

Elfer, Goldschmied, and Selleck (2013) concluded three key factors undervalued professional care work with children:

- The dominance on the narrative of being 'school ready' and preparing for school education, with little focus on the affective domains of learning and development.
- The persistent dominance of the maternal discourse (McDowall Clark and Bayliss, 2012) which characterises skill and proficiency as 'natural' and 'innate' attributes.
- The emotional connection to young children is central to the role (Elfer et al., 2013). The maternal discourse stems from a view of child care as providing a substitute mother role, a gendered image that assumes research and education is unnecessary to undertake the role and it either comes 'naturally' or, if not, experience will prevail.

Areas such as tuning in to children can be helpful in unexpected ways, because they often express emotions that are challenging to manage and with the support of the key person they can share their feelings. Tuning in can also be advantageous as a reflection tool for key persons to acknowledge infants who are less expressive and more insular in conveying their emotions (Mooney, 2010). Vallotton (2009) studied whether infants can influence their quality of care and concluded that infant communicative gestures predicted caregiver responsiveness. Therefore, infants and children influenced the behaviour of the caregivers.

Children, Practitioners, and TO

Given that parents, day care providers, and children themselves use various means of providing the child with a sense of security and continuity, children's use of objects is especially important. This is when children are under stressful situations or vulnerable states, such as in unfamiliar environments, when upset, ill, or tired. The favoured objects come to serve a comforting, anxiety-reducing function for the child. Despite some notions regarding the nature and functions that object attachments serve for young children, the sources for this developmental phenomenon have not been empirically studied widely, leaving the factors that contribute to children's use of non-social objects for comfort not well understood. It is generally considered to be part of normal development (Winnicott, 1953; Bowlby, 1969), and the ability to rely on an object that is accessible and manipulated by the child is thought to have a facilitative influence in anxiety-evoking situations (Passman, 1977). It is, however, not an essential developmental step, as many children do not develop such emotional dependencies toward non-social objects, and there may be some less optimal long-term associations related with this behaviour (Fortuna et al., 2014).

Voice Vignette: Reflections of the TO

Examples of Transitional Objects and Objects of Attachment: A Pink Blanket

- I have a soft pink blanket.
- I love wrapping it around me and taking it to bed with me.
- I chose the initial cuddle, it was huge. It was cut down as it frayed and I still had parts of it, one section stayed with me.
- Then my grandmother replaced it, and it was never the same.
- I had it to sleep with.
- Its texture was nice to rub on my face. I took it everywhere with me.
- I could cuddle up with it or stroke it on my face and it smelt like home and my mum.
- When it was washed, I had to have a T-shirt of my mum's for the night to sleep and I found it upsetting.

- It was a comfort to me and was my love.
- I grew out of it at 11 when going to senior school.

Transitional Objects and Covid

In 2020 the Department for Education (DfE) (now withdrawn) wrote, 'Because early childhood is the most significant time for cognitive, social and emotional development, early years settings will be able to re-open to all pre-school children from June 2020' (DfE, 2020: n.p.). Three- and four-year-olds were the first to return to nurseries followed by younger age groups. To help formal day care settings to prepare, the DfE issued guidance which included reducing group sizes and keeping children in small groups without mixing with others as well as staggered break and lunch times, drop offs, and pickups. It also advised nurseries to increase the frequency of cleaning of toys and play equipment and 'remove' soft furnishings, soft toys, and toys that are hard to clean (DfE, 2020). There was also the suggestion to actively discourage soft toys from being brought into settings by the children.

According to David Wright, co-owner of Paint Pots Nurseries in Southampton during this time, wrote that the ban on teddies in settings potentially makes it harder to 'manage children's distress at leaving parents' (Learner, 2020). He was concerned that, after months of being at home, children would need a period of transition to nursery and they are often helped to settle in by bringing their cuddly toy from home. At the time he said, 'When our children return, won't they need a teddy to cuddle and yet we are being directed to remove them'. He did not believe a blanket ban on soft toys and furnishings was appropriate.

> We have to ask questions about the quality of life. If this persists, as we are told to expect, will we be raising our children from now on in individual isolated chalked squares on hard floors, devoid of human touch and familiar objects for comfort?

He also expressed concern that children will 'feel as though they are being punished', and said 'What sort of existence is that?' Pauline Scott, owner of Lullaby Lane Nurseries in Scotland, also highlighted her concerns about banning soft toys during the pandemic, and although she acknowledged it was guidance only for England, she also felt this advice would be taken too literally across the United Kingdom (Learner, 2020).

As we have moved from the pandemic of 2020 and the report is now a historical document, their comforters need to reflect practices that have changed and also how the nexus of the past informs the present. In some areas regarding admission, the use of toys and equipment, altered during the pandemic, has continued to 'live on'.

> I have claimed that when we witness an infant's employment of a transitional object, the first not-me possession, we are witnessing both the child's

first use of a symbol and the first experience of play ... The use of an object symbol symbolises the union of two now separate things, baby and mother, at the point in time and space of the initiation of their state of separateness.

(Winnicott, 1971: 130)

A consensus across settings is that TO contribute to an important social and emotional function of daily life. By focusing on this area, the implication is that more understanding about TO is needed through which children can actively share their feelings and collaboratively be part of their own care practices. I have suggested a model as a starting point whereby settings can begin to reflect and discuss how TO are perceived and experienced by the children in the setting. The model is not intended to be prescriptive but rather outline some of the main themes discussed in the book that may be of practical help, serving as part of group supervision or team meetings.

Application to Practice and What We Can Learn about Transitional Objects: An Approach in Working with Children

In supporting clear aims in settings, children can feel valued and listened to. These aims should be to:

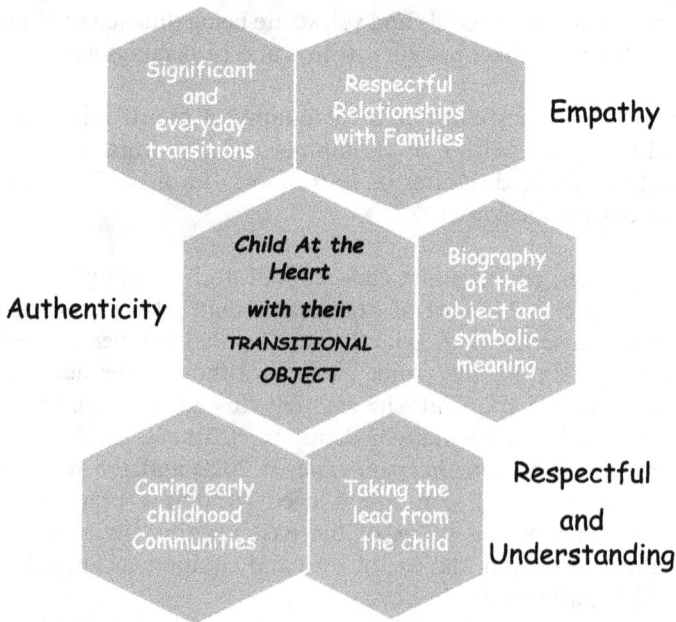

Figure 6.1 A caring approach with children and transitional objects. Policies in early years settings to develop a relational approach and acceptance of Transitional Objects.

- Acknowledge the problem and your child's feelings.
- Encourage your child to describe the problem to you.
- Ask your child for ideas on solutions to the problem.
- Allow enough time for your child to solve the problem independently.
- When your child is too frustrated or on the verge of abandoning his or her own ideas, offer your help (Rosneath Primary School and ELC, 2023b).

Approaches to Supporting Attachments in Practice

Zeedyk (2020) captured two key areas that are insightful when thinking about attachment and anxiety. She defined these as sabre tooth tigers and teddy bears. The book provides an insight into the science of attachment and contempoary relationships. The young child may fear many things unknown to their carer, such as being alone or when adults invade their space. The 'Sabre Tooth Tiger' is a symbol for carers as a survival mode in thinking about infant's anxieties and reliance on them to feel safe. The second insight from the science of attachment is the value about comfort and this is symbolised as 'Teddy Bears' as a way of providing reassurance. Responsive attention from parents and practitioners is a way of supporting young children to develop an 'internal teddy bear'. This also supports the growth of self-regulation that can be helpful as the child grows, supporting their emotional well-being. In thinking about how TO are navigated by the child, a consideration about how they are approached and supported with practitioners in a formal day care setting is therefore valuable.

By supporting the use of objects of attachment as they re-emerge into settings, their TO can become weaved into and central to policy and practice in a bid to develop well-being and create flourishing environments.

Voice Vignette: Policy and Practice

In April 2023, Dr Susanne Zeedyk visited Rosneath, a primary school in Scotland, to observe the introduction and impact of their new Teddy Bear Policy, developed as part of their school policies.

The introduction of a Teddy Bear policy works alongside the behavioural and relationships policies. In practice it involves teddy bears for each class but is also about creating space for children to talk and be comforted. There is the emphasis on the learning environment being increasingly focused towards developing children's confidence, empathy, and self-esteem whilst they are at school. Although many schools and formal day care settings have had specialist training to be trauma informed, this school has extended it further by introducing and implementing the new policy, also informed from an understanding about Adverse Childhood Experiences (ACEs) and Understanding Trauma (Zeedyk, 2008).

In developing the approach, the teddy bears are included in the school, widening the need beyond formal day care, which often only accommodates children up to four years old, until they attend school in England. By creating a school inclusive Teddy Bear Policy, they can be included to create a special area with benches and garden space for the children to use. The Bear benches are available so the children can sit and chat to friends and do outdoor activities. It is also hoped that if a child is feeling emotional, they can sit on a bench and indicate how they are feeling, perhaps seeking a hug or a friend to talk to. It would also be an area the children can in time further develop with their own thoughts and ideas. The children's voices are central with the ideas conceived of a Teddy Bear Policy, informed from the research completed by Zeedyk on attachment about Sabre Tooth Tigers and Teddy Bears (Rosneath Primary School and ELC, 2023b).

In other settings the United Nations Convention on the Rights of the Child (UNCRC) has been directly referred to as they have set out to reshape their policies and inform the setting about their responsibilities to make sure that all children enjoy their rights. It is also a way of connecting and protecting children to develop their potential. This includes empowering children to exercise their rights and to become responsible, rights-respecting citizens (Bainsford Primary School, 2023).

Whilst I appreciate many of the teddies may not be considered Transitional Objects it certainly provides a more accepting way of creating a more post-humanist view about education and the value objects symbolise to young children. In moving beyond the youngest community and the assumption TO are not necessary in middle childhood, this adds to the growing research about the child being viewed developmentally and individually rather than according to chronological age and the expectations around it. For some children their personal toys or favourite objects may also serve as their TO. The objects, encouraged to be brought to the setting, are a way of connecting home with nursery. By accepting the relationship between the object and the child, transitions to and from settings may be less stressful and encourage children to be able to make their own choices about what makes them feel secure and safe. This also encourages a move away from some of the pandemic practices about leaving toys and objects at home.

Examples of Transitional Objects and Objects of Attachment: Home Teddy

Often a teddy in day care was used as a home, nursery teddy. The teddy would go home and spend the week with the child. The teddy adventures would be recorded in a book and for many of the children I worked with the teddy become a significant and important part of their world, a non-human part of their world, in a way, perhaps like a pet. It was always carefully looked after, and the child would take the lead in it, both at the setting and when they took it home.

Opportunities for Play and the Practitioner's Role

The affordance of playing reveals how children are capable, given reasonably good and stable surroundings, of developing a personal way of life and eventually becoming a whole human welcomed by the world at large. By being allowed to play, they learn to trust in the environment and have the capacity to be alone. In the presence of someone else, playing involves the body because of manipulation of objects and their interactions. Winnicott (1953) believes there is creativity involved and the individual in spontaneous action experiences both creativity and cognitive development as they move towards independence to engagement in a significant interchange with the world (Winnicott, 1958).

As researcher and practitioner, I have been very fortunate in having opportunities to reflect on and observe the way pedagogy has been approached with infants through an educare approach. Pedagogy is not only about the how and why of what early years' educators do in their professional roles, but also extends to the way practitioners as key persons engage with the expectations presented to them in their day care setting. Children learn best in atmospheres that provide a stimulating and prepared environment where they learn from their own perspectives (Lilley, 1967). In the setting, time to plan areas for children to choose how they want to engage with their emotions and be cared for by a listening and observant practitioner is essential for development and well-being to occur (Davis and Wallbridge, 1991: 61).

Voice Vignette 1: The Book and the Words in the Book

Gina Goody (2012) provides one child's use of a story as a Transitional Object (TO), and it is a fascinating case study account moving beyond what we often assume are the objects associated with TO. It is also a good illustration about how TO have been observed in practice. It is a case study of her grandson, Zack, who is four years old, and his engagement with the picture book *Clown* by Quentin Blake during an emotional period in his life. Zack's engagement with picture books has confirmed Goody's assumption about how important picture books are for both the affective and the cognitive domains of children's developing, and revealed how TO in many guises can be beneficial during turbulent times.

During the time the case study project was undertaken by Goody, the birth of Zack's sister was imminent. It was during this period that Zack developed a profound attachment to a wordless picture book, created by Quentin Blake and titled *Clown*. Goody documented his relationship with the text through interpreting it as a Transitional Object. Picture books are usually the first text and the first form of literature to which children are introduced in the form of board books, novelty books, and pop-up books.

Throughout an intense and emotional period in Zack's life, Goody made entries in her journal reflecting and exploring the relationship with the picture book. The book seemed to help as Zack transitioned from one place to another. She documented the value of the book extensively as a literate source and how the contents and the objects themselves were significant. She also reflected on the position Zack was in regarding his family dynamics and how this was transitioning.

Voice Vignette 2: Owl Babies (Waddell and Bensen, 1992)

This is another book that links with attachment and bonding within an owl family.

> 'Where has Mummy gone?'
> 'She'll bring us mice and things that are nice!', said Sarah.
> 'I suppose so', said Percy.
> 'I want my Mummy', said Bill.
> …
> 'What's all the fuss? You knew I'd come back!'
> 'I knew it!', said Sarah.
> 'I knew it!', said Percy.
> 'I love my Mummy!', said Bill.

This story was a firm favourite with a child I cared for. The child had begun attending a setting and was feeling quite anxious. Each morning, as part of the routine, he would want the book read to him and, although he had memorised the words, would continue to have it as part of his settling in routine. His mother would personalise the book and change the names which he enjoyed, and this extended his association with the book. The mother was also at home with the birth of a second child and was working. The story within is about how the mother owl goes and they are unsure where she is. The narrative follows that they get anxious, with the youngest being quite literal in saying he wants his mummy, the older two trying to justify why she has gone. The ending is when the mother returns. It was the story in the topic within that had meaning attachment and transition particularly (Figure 6.2).

Voice Vignette 3: Transition Objects and Film

A further illustration was a child named Ben. He would hold an Elsa doll frequently and carry it with him wherever he went. He had watched the film *Frozen* and it was noted that, like many other children, the imagery, music, and story of the film had captured his imagination. However, it was observed that, rather than the doll itself being the Transition Object that he carried around, it was more about the hair on the doll. The hair was long and the feeling and stroking of the hair seemed symbolic. He would also stroke his mother's long hair and often had a strand as he sucked his thumb. His peer was a girl with very long hair of the same colour, and

Figure 6.2 Stories, objects and transitions.

this was his 'best friend'. He sometimes pulled strands from his own hair, and it seemed to be a comforting medium as he transitioned in spaces and states. The transitional time to lie down and rest was often the time when needed to stroke and pull gently at his doll's hair and his own, or his carer's. The longer, the better the character. The doll, Elsa, seemed to be an object that he could use when human hair was not readily available.

As we know, a child assumes, when the parent is gone, they are gone forever, and feels abandoned and traumatised; however, a sense of equilibrium is achieved on their return. Children who are unable to hold their parents in their mind just think they have gone. Transitions can trigger an emotional response to the upheaval of transitioning from one space to another and this can be from simply sitting on the carpet to moving into the nursery garden. These are things, as adults, we assume children are compliant with and we are almost dismissive of their movements. From the child's perspective, this evokes extreme distress when experiencing transitions and reminds us of the material world they engage in. This may also involve people and relationships in the child's life and as they grow to keeping their parents or carers in mind, they become real, and therefore the child is saturated with despair when they leave. In supporting the child there is a need for sensitive, caring, and supportive adults to be able to comfort and alleviate the grief borne by the child due to abandonment, by offering loving gestures when they are ready to accept them and creating an emotionally holding space for the child.

This is also a reminder that Winnicott's theory about TO is not about the object that is transitional, but the object represents the infant's transition from a stage of being merged with the parent to a state of being in relation to the parent or something outside but inseparable (Winnicott, 1971: 19).

Transitional Objects provide the hope that both the physical reality of the book and the psychological experience of the text can be interpreted as TO. This was the relationship that Zack discovered through his multiple readings of *Clown* and the *Owl Babies*.

Winnicott (1960) also described a boy who appears to show sorrow with decreased happiness at the arrival of a new baby brought home. For him, the new baby was suddenly a new reality in his world, and this was causing him decreased happiness. Primarily, this was his position as third person in relation to his parents, whereas previously he had taken centre stage and was the central part of his parent's love (Winnicott, 1991, 2016).

Goody (2012) described her grandson's behaviour and emotional connections to the book during nightly readings. She was reflecting on this time and period, documenting the way Zack used his eye contact, scanning the environment as well as the book. The book offered an imaginary space that enabled the facilitating or holding environment to be brought into being. By her presence, it was also a facilitating environment, a physical and emotional space in which the 'good-enough' mother (in this case the grandmother) holds the child both literally and figuratively (Arnold, 2012).

Goody was able to capture the richness of the relationship and the way the book, as an object but also the images and text within, served a purpose as a TO. As an educator, she highlights the value for resisting the reductive style of learning and the consideration about what has been excluded and why it needs to be acknowledged. She considered the relationship between thought and language as being crucial, so the language children develop empowers them. The case study also emphasised the intensity of the relationships that children have with books and books have with children. By including the personal experiences to the world of the text, Goody advocates for the child to be able to access the TO when they need it and settings to include the continual availability of a child's TO. The children should be empowered by the TO rather than the TO taken away, restricted in use, and governed by the adults caring for the children (Goody, 2012).

A Final Note

This chapter's central focus is the justification about how TO can be part of a child's world within day care and in school. It includes some innovative practices and the different forms of TO chosen by the children themselves and their rationale for choice. It bridges policy with practice and I hope it evokes a fruitful, reflective consideration about how TO could be part of the settings they work in.

References

Arnold, C. (2012) *Improving Your Reflective Practise through Stories of Practitioner Research*. London: Routledge.

Bain, A. and Barnett, L. (1986) *The Design of a Day Care System in a Nursery Setting for Children under Five.* London: Tavistock Institute of Human Relations Document number 2T347.

Bainsford Primary School (2023) How we protect children's rights with the UN Convention on the Rights of the Child. Available at: www.bainsford.falkirk.sch.uk/uncrc/uncrc.html

Boniface, D. and Graham, P. (1979) The three year old and his attachment to a special soft object. *Journal of Child Psychology and Psychiatry*, 20: 217–224. https://doi.org/10.1111/j.1469-7610.1979.tb00505

Bowlby, J. (1969) *Attachment and Loss, Vol. I: Attachment.* New York. Basic Books.

Dahlberg, G., Moss, P., and Pence, A. (1999) *Beyond Quality in Early Childhood Education and Care: Postmodern Perspectives.* London: Falmer Press.

Davis, M. and Wallbridge, D. (1991) *Boundary and Space: An Introduction to the Work of Dr Winnicott.* London: Karnac Books.

DfE (2020) Action for Early Years and Childcare Providers During the Covid19 Pandemic. Available at: https://assets.publishing.service.gov.uk/government/uploads/system/uploads/attachment_data/file/1096889/_WITHDRAWN__20220223_EY_guidance.pdf

Elfer, P., Goldschmied, E., and Selleck, D. (2013) *Key Persons in the Nursery Building Relationships for Quality Provision.* London: David Fulton Books.

Fortuna, K., Baor, L., Israel, S., Abadi, A., and Knafo, A. (2014) Attachment to inanimate objects and early childcare: A twin study. *Frontiers in Psychology*, 22 (5): 486. https://doi.org/10.3389/fpsyg.2014.00486

Gaddini, R. and Gaddini, E. (1970) Transitional objects and the process of individuation: a study in three different social groups. *Journal of the American Academy of Child & Adolescent Psychiatry*, 9: 347–365.

Goddard, C. (2014) More than just teddy bears: Transitional objects allow a child's inherent sense of self to emerge. *Psychology Today*, July 15, 2014. Available at: www.psychologytoday.com/gb/blog/the-guest-room/201407/more-just-teddy-bears.

Goleman, D. (1995) *Emotional Intelligence: Why It Can Matter More than IQ.* London: Bloomsbury.

Goody, G. (2012) One child's use of a story as a transitional object. In C. Arnold, *Improving Your Reflective Practice through Stories of Practitioner Research.* London: Routledge.

Learner, S. (2020) COVID-19: Ban on teddies in nurseries will make it hard to 'manage children's distress at leaving parents. *Day Nurseries.* Available at: www.daynurseries.co.uk/news/article.cfm/id/1626094/banning-teddies-nurseries-covid-19-risks-manage-distress

Lehman, E. B., Denham, S. A., Moser, M. H., and Reeves, S. L. (1992) Soft object and pacifier attachments in young children: The role of security of attachment to the mother. *Journal of Child Psychology and Psychiatry*, 33: 1205–1215. https://doi.org/10.1111/j.1469-7610.1992.tb00939

Lilley, I. (1967) *Friedrich Froebel: A Selection from His Writings.* Cambridge: Cambridge University Press.

Litt, C. J. (1981) Children's attachment to transitional objects: A study of two pediatric populations. *American Journal of Orthopsychiatry*, 51: 131–139. https://doi.org/10.1111/j.1939-0025.1981.tb01355.x

Manning-Morton, J. and Thorpe, M. (2003) *Key Times for Play: The First Three Years.* Milton Keynes: Open University Press.

McDowall Clark, R. and Bayliss, S. (2012) 'Wasted down there': policy and practice with the under-threes. *Early Years: An International Journal of Research and Development*, 32 (2): 229–242.

Mooney, C. (2010) *Theories of Attachment*. St Paul: Redleaf Press.

Passman, R. H. (1977) Providing attachment objects to facilitate learning and reduce distress: Effects of mothers and security blankets. *Developmental Psychology*, 13: 25–28. https://doi.org/10.1037/0012-1649.13.1.25

Rosneath Primary School and ELC (2023a) Teddy bear policy. Available at: www.rosnea th.argyll-bute.sch.uk/teddy-bear-policy/

Rosneath Primary School and ELC (2023b) Family engagement. Available at: https:// www.rosneath.argyll-bute.sch.uk/family-engagement/

Rutter, M. (1985) Resilience in the face of adversity: protective factors and resistance to psychiatric disorder. *British Journal of Psychiatry*, 147: 598–611. htps://doi.org/ 10.1192/bjp.147.6.598

Society for Research in Child Development (SRCD) (2023) Oral history project. Available at: www.srcd.org/about-us/who-we-are/oral-history-project (accessed October 14, 2022).

Triebenbacher, S. L. and Tegano, D. W. (1993) Children's use of transitional objects during daily separations from significant caregivers. *Perceptual and Motor Skills*, 76: 89–90. https://doi.org/10.2466/pms.1993.76.1.89

Vallotton, C. (2009) Do infants influence their quality of care? Infants' communicative gestures predict caregivers' responsiveness. *Infant Behavior and Development*, 32: 351–365.

Van IJzendoorn, M. H., Goossens, F. A., Tavecchio, L. W. C., Vergeer, M. M, and Hubbard, F. O. A. (1983) Attachment to soft objects: Its relationship with attachment to the mother and with thumbsucking. *Child Psychiatry & Human Development*, 14: 97–105. https://doi.org/10.1007/BF00707674

Waddell, M. and Bensen, P. (1992) *Owl Babies*. London: Walker Books.

Winnicott, D. W. (1953) Transitional objects and transitional phenomena: A study of the first not-me possession. *International Journal of Psychoanalysis*, 34: 89–97.

Winnicott, D. W. (1958) The capacity to be alone. *International Journal of Psychoanalysis*, 39: 416–420.

Winnicott, D. W. (1960) The theory of the parent–infant relationship. In *The Maturational Processes and the Facilitating Environment*. New York: International Universities Press.

Winnicott, D. W. (1971) The use of an object and relating through identifications. In *Playing and Reality*. New York: Basic Books.

Winnicott, D. W. (1987) *Babies and Mothers*. London: Meryl Lawrence.

Winnicott, D. W. (1991) *Playing and Reality*. London: Psychology Press.

Winnicott, D. W. (2016) *The Collected Works of D. W. Winnicott* (Vol. 12). Oxford: Oxford University Press.

Zeedyk, S. (2008) Infant buggies may undermine child development. Observational study, University of Dundee.

Zeedyk, S. (2020) *Sabre Tooth Tigers and Teddy Bears: The Connected Baby Guide to Attachment*. Dundee: Connected Baby Ltd. Available at: https://connectedbaby.net

Chapter 7

A Cross-Disciplinary Approach to Transitional Objects

Symbolic, Transitional, and Sentimental Objects

This chapter explores the biography of symbolic, transitional, and sentimental objects and how objects can reveal understandings about individuals' past and present lives. This will be critically explored within differing contexts and by different professionals to widen the discussion about Transitional Objects. The various and shifting ideas about objects being meaning makers and personalised will be discussed. The latter part of the chapter will then specifically focus on childhood and personal objects that have transitional meanings and a model that could be explored and discussed within formal day care settings.

Transitional Objects today and Winnicott

In 1953, Donald Winnicott presented his idea of Transitional Objects (TO) and how they play a role in children's development. Children's ability to attach themselves to objects displays a phase of ego development, and later assists in the child developing a sense of self (Litt, 1986). Winnicott focused on defining the transition from how an infant's first in-mouth activities, such as thumb sucking, as well as the developing reliance to a teddy or other object for comfort (Winnicott, 1953). Transitional phenomena were established through Winnicott's observation of objects that gain importance to the child. Winnicott examined a personal pattern that children develop with a self-selected object that is not contained within themselves. He evaluated that when a child connects a common experience with an auto-erotic experience, for example, using a piece of cloth or blanket and sucking on it or sucking on thumb and babbling, this reveals the visibility of transitional phenomena. These objects are separate from the body, but also not completely recognised as part of the external reality. The phenomena are during times such as when the child is going to sleep, or moving to a new setting – a defence against anxiety or depression. The use of the TO therefore revels the phenomena. Winnicott suggested that the pattern of transitional phenomena begins to emerge between 6 and 12 months of age. This object is valued by the child and taken most places that the child goes. Winnicott (1953) also notes there

DOI: 10.4324/9781003296669-10

were no observable differences when considering gender in the choice of TO and the object never changes unless done so by the child. The objects hold so much symbolic value for the child that it becomes the child's reality. Even while children may not yet be able to cognitively understand symbolism, the object is able to show the beginnings of symbolism.

Children's Perceptions of Transitional Objects

Lehman and colleagues (1992) examined the relationship between child and Transitional Object from the perspective of the child. The goal of the study was to understand the child's beliefs about their TO and where these beliefs come from (Lehman et al., 1992). Eighty-one children between the ages of four and eight years were interviewed. The results revealed that 55% of the children had TO. Children discussed the characteristics of the object, the object's history, why they used them, whether the parent(s) encouraged or discouraged use of TO, and the children's own attitudes towards them (Lehman et al., 1992). They revealed that the most prevalent topic was the texture of the TO. The texture was discussed in terms of their softness, furriness, or smoothness (Lehman et al., 1992). The children also described the cuddliness, smell, colour, and temperature of the TO. The history of the TO revealed that most of the children believed they had possessed the object for a long time, receiving them when they were a baby. All the TO in the study had been named and over half of the participants said that they named the object. Over half (55%) of the TO attached to children were used during bedtime or naptime. Emotional states whereby a TO was needed included when they were sad, sleepy, scared, angry, and lastly, happy. The children stated that they wanted their TO because it would give them control over the situation because the TO does what it is told to do and they can express freely to their TO (Lehman et al., 1992).

Parent's Perceptions of Transitional Objects

Triebenbacher and Tegano (1993) examined the attitudes and perceptions that parents have about their child's use of Transitional Objects. Mothers and fathers varied in their views of their child wanting or needing their TO, with mothers responding that their child wanted or needed their object in more situations than fathers. However, both mothers and fathers agreed that their child wanted or needed their TO when they went to sleep, felt tired or upset, or were not feeling well. While parents agreed on scenarios where the object was wanted, they also agreed on scenarios where the child should not take their TO with them. Parents perceived that children's TO should not be taken to church, or out in public locations, or to school. Triebenbacher's study revealed that, overall, both mothers and fathers understand the significance of their child's TO, and the importance of the child's attachment. Furthermore, parent's own use of TO in their childhood was related to their acceptance of their child's TO. Lehman et al. (1992) examined mothers' perspective of their child's TO. The findings revealed that 68% of their children, according to the mothers, had established an attachment with their object before the age of 18 months (Lehman et al., 1992). Maternal attitudes revealed that most mothers were pleased about their child's use of TO, and believed the most important attributes of the selected object were its texture and softness (Lehman et al., 1996). Mothers perceived that TO were most useful when the child was sleeping, separated from the parents, and mastering challenging tasks. Parents in both studies understood the importance of TO when the child was going to sleep, either at bedtime or naptime.

In Scherer and Norman's (2023) study on exploring the sleeping voices of the child within popular parenting book. They reported on much how the child's voice was considered and included during night-time routines within a selection of popular parenting books aimed to support parents with children between the ages of two and five years. Predominately the voice of the sleep-book authors were read as expert-dominated, the platform being their parenting book, marketed as 'authentic' and successful in promoting positive sleep. Interestingly, the comfort object associated with sleep was superficially mentioned with no reference to it as a significant buffer to sleep or significant reference as a TO.

A review of empirical literature revealed that TO served as a positive coping mechanism for children in a variety of emotional and physical states, including but not limited to:

1   new and novel experiences;
2   sleep;
3   child care;
4   medical settings and shared common dimensions (Leitner, 2016).

The concept of the TO is therefore an important one beyond early education and could be valuable for paediatricians and nursing staff to consider. Currently it is routine to ask the parents of a child being admitted to hospital whether the child has a special toy or blanket and to ensure the parent does not forget it in the drama of the admission. Paediatrician's have anecdotally said they advise mothers who had to temporarily leave their children, to give the child something they know belonged to the mother such as a purse, scarf, or even keys as a way of knowing they will return (Isaacs and Isaacs, 2014).

Children and TO in Hospital

Children often experience medical interventions and hospitalisations at some point during their early years. These medical settings can be unfamiliar external environments for children and may require some separations from their established attachment figures, with the potential for the environment to be extremely stressful. By identifying effective coping strategies for children who are experiencing stress, the use of a TO may be a valuable aid to reducing stress. Currently, there is limited research examining children's use of TO in health care settings or how child life specialists advocate for children's use of TO in health care settings. In Leitner's (2016) study, specialists were examined in their views about how they advocate for the use of TO in paediatric health care settings. The study also explored the current policies in medical settings that guide the use of TO, as well as the practices of 'child life specialists' when they encounter a child with a TO. Results of the study revealed that only five of the 24 participants reported that their setting did not have any policies guiding the use of TO. Most participants reported that they felt mostly knowledgeable about TO and believed them to be extremely important in stressful settings. Overall, participants revealed that they were willing to advocate for children's need to have access to TO in health care settings (Leitner, 2016).

The Life Course and TO: Parents and TO in Hospitals

Whilst Transitional Objects are often viewed through the children's lens, it is also worth reflecting on how parents have used objects in their emotional transitions during their life course. Parents who experience a perinatal loss often leave the hospital with empty arms and no tangible mementos to validate the parenting experience. Opportunities to create parenting experiences

Figure 7.1 A reminder of my hospital doll and that it remains in its original dress and the hair is the same.

with TO exist following their infant's death. Recommendations exist and are well supported by leading neonatal and perinatal nursing and medicine organisations for the use of TO to facilitate healthy grieving when parents experience perinatal loss. Transitional Objects are mementos that validate the meaning of parenthood – even if the physical act of parenting was brief. Nursing and medical staff have significant roles in guiding parents to a healthy state of bereavement and ultimately managing long-term grief, with TO (LeDuff et al., 2017).

Voice Vignette: Getting to Know the Transitional Objects

For Winnicott (1960) it was much more about the transitional phenomena than the state of the child. The the object itself. symbolised the transitional spaces in extending this. By understandingthe object and how it is used and navigated by the child, an appreciation of the biography of the object may support deeper understanding of the child.

The Cuddle Cloth: The Biography of the Cloth

We often think about the TO in terms of the transition being central. However, the object itself can also be symbolic and take many forms. I have created a narrative to try and explain and illustrate this further, from my observations of children with their TO.

The Story of the Cloth

The cuddle cloth was not always a cuddle cloth. It was a blanket large enough to cover a cot and encase a baby. The blanket had grey stars on it and tassels around the side. Each night the blanket was lifted by the parent and rested on their baby, the corners tucked in as the baby slept. As the baby woke, they pulled and wiggled around the blanket, pulling on its corners with warm chubby fingers. The tassels were revealed, and the baby rolled over and sucked their thumb and with their fingers stroked the tassels across their cheeks as they slowly woke for the day.

The parent would enter, and the blanket would be lifted and gently rested on the edge of the cot bed. The parent would gaze at the blanket as she lifted the baby and recollect the time when the blanket was made by an elder in the family, in another country. The blanket had been flown over as a special gift.

As time went on, the corners of the blanket began to be pulled and were slightly torn by the weak stitches. The cloth became fragmented and torn, parts coming away; the corner triangle was cut away and the fragmented piece was given to the child. They could now lift a part of the blanket as they too were lifted out of the cot. They held the blanket, sniffed, and rubbed it as they moved beyond the sleep space associated with the blanket. The blanket corner now had an opportunity to be part of the child's world. The blanket piece was screwed up in their hand.

The blanket smells of the child, but also the parent. The blanket was a symbol of love and separation by the parent made for a purpose and flown from a different culture, with colour and materials with associated meanings for the family.

The blanket was a symbol of love and separation, a piece of home, their parent, and a safe base to physically hold their world literally in the palm of their hand.

Public to Personal

A Transitional Object tends to be chosen in the first six months of life and to sometimes have qualities reminiscent of the mother. It is soft, stroked, cuddled and bitten, and, on a symbolic level, it links to maternal care. Sarner (2018, n.p.) recorded voices of adults who possessed a TO and provides a historical record of their meaning to the owners.

> I was born just after the war when things were tight and because my mother couldn't afford a teddy bear, one of her nursing colleagues made Ted out of the only material she had – a kind of green hessian, with black felt eyepatches. At present, he looks very dishevelled.

Ted has been in Graham's life for seven decades. 'He was a very, very significant part of my childhood for a while and he's part of me.' Until Graham was about eight, he chatted to Ted every night in bed. 'I can remember I really thought I talked to him. He's a superb listener'.

He would tell him significant things that had happened that day, as a way of sorting things out in his mind, before falling asleep hugging Ted (Sarner, 2018).

In Winnicott's theory, these possessions are about more than comfort: they lead to play, which is fundamental to the development of a healthy mind. In what he calls 'the intermediate space' that opens between mother and baby, occupied and stretched by the TO, the child's imagination and creativity grow. 'It is good to remember always that playing itself is a therapy', Winnicott (1953) wrote.

A further example from Sarner's (2018) report on TO was that Anindita Roulet's need for her Kaporji TO remains as strong as ever. Born in London but having moved to India to live with her grandparents in the east Indian city of Jamshedpur when she was one year old, because her parents were struggling to manage, Anindita has no memories of it, but says 'I've seen some photos and I certainly look like I was having a whale of a time. It's quite an idyllic life and a deeply affectionate family. I suspect I was spoilt rotten.'

She explains how her Kaporji, which she translates from Bengali as Sir Cloth, came to be. 'During that year in India, I slept beside my grandmother every night and she wore a white cotton sari loosely wrapped around her. It was the train of this sari I held on to as I slept.'

When Roulet's parents came to bring her back to London, the separation from her grandparents was painful for the two-year-old. But her grandmother packed a couple of cotton saris in her suitcase and Roulet's mother cut out a large square for her to take to bed.

'After one piece disintegrated, another would replace it – always a piece of my granny's sari and no one else's', she says. 'My mum would stick pieces in the washing machine to get it softer and softer, so that when I needed a replacement it wasn't too stiff.'

Her memory of the year spent with her grandmother faded, but her attachment to her Kaporji did not. When a sari ran out, her grandmother would send more, or they would be collected during visits back to India every few years (Sarner, 2018).

'I'm still sleeping with it. I know it's ridiculous, at 46, but I can't quite give it up,' she says. 'It's very soft and I hold it in a fist in my right hand. My fingers sink into it and it feels really reassuring. Most nights, I will lose it for a moment as I loosen my grip in my sleep, but I always retrieve it and wake up with it in the morning,' says Roulet.

She did not remain as close with her grandmother, whom she saw only every few years but they always shared a bond, although they never spoke of it, 'I'm very grateful for the fact that I have this connection, this thread – several threads – that run through our lives together' (Sarner, 2018, n.p.).

The Object and the Significance of the Inanimate

An object such as a teddy bear is like a little portable piece of a parent that a child can take everywhere. As a child forms a bond with their teddy, they learn to associate the same feel-good emotions that they get from being around their parents. They can then feel more confident and comfortable with their bear close for those inevitable moments when familiar faces aren't around. Perry (2022) also found that children who were excluded in social situations found it easier to try to engage with their peers after holding a teddy bear. One important way that teddy bears and other TO aid in a child's journey to independence was by letting them practise being in a nurturing role. When a child had the opportunity to care for another in the same way, they could reinforce what they had learned, such as tucking their teddy into bed, serving them dinner, or taking them out to play. Teddy bears therefore provide them with a trusted, loving companion with which they can feel safe practicing. The objects are a way for them to practice and reinforce important life skills, self-sooth and feel the parent's love even when the parent is not nearby (Bears for Humanity, 2021; Sarner, 2018).

Conducting Early Years Research Through an Alternative Lens when Reflecting on Transitional Objects

In rhizoanalysis, the focus is an approach to research conditioned by a reality in which Deleuze and Guattari (2014) disrupt representation, interpretation, and subjectivity. Thinking about Transitional Objects, theoretically and their practical applications, becomes a lens to potentially examining how individuals conceptualise and reflect on the way TO are analysed and understood (Olsson, 2009; Sellars, 2013).

By exploring the voices of children, it also provokes further analytical considerations for professionals to consider and question TO and how they have been analysed in studies. From my own thinking, it disrupts my existing knowledge about TO and raises questions such as:

- How and why TO are researched less, interpreted, and sometimes deemed differently in middle childhood?
- What is the continuous as well as transient relationship with an inanimate object – sentimental or a TO?
- Why we culturally consider some spaces and places for children to have and others less so?
- What we mean by healthy development and if having a TO in late adulthood is healthy?
- The loss and separation of a TO and how it is often trivialised by those around but often with significant impact on the child themselves through to adulthood.

Rhizoanalysis proposes to abandon the given and invent different ways of thinking about and doing within our lived experience as well as in research. Thinking of the material world around me what might happen when I read and interpret studies and engage with material and people through an alternative lens. Rhizoanalysis, for me is about altering the way I research and perceive the world as a professional working with children. It affords multiple and various lenses to tackle issues in early childhood, in education and care, as well as through research, as a multi-layered, complex, and messy process (Deleuze and Guattari, 2014).

The Biography of the Object and Connections to the TO

Attachment to objects is driven by a deeply rooted behavioural and hormonal response which is an extension of our innate mammalian attachment system (Bowlby, 1969). This attachment system leads us to seek out attachment figures who provide us with feelings of comfort and security (Bowlby, 1969; Gillath et al., 2016). The secure attachment figure provides two benefits: a safe haven, and a secure base (Bowlby, 1988). The former of these encompasses the feeling and knowledge that we are cared for, and that we have someone to go to for comfort, while the latter gives us the confidence to explore our environment, knowing that support remains available (Bell and Spikins 2018). Interactions with attachment figures affect one's 'internal working model' or 'script' about the way the world is viewed, the way we view ourselves, and the way we expect to be treated by others.

Thus, attachment security fundamentally structures how we perceive and relate to the world around us.

In appreciating this process, attachment objects, often presented initially as gifts, can be very varied in form and whilst sensory qualities such as warmth and softness are important in children's attachment objects, they are less essential to adults. Some attachment objects are soft and 'huggable', for example a toy guinea pig, described in simple terms as 'multi-coloured yellow, brown, white and very soft'.

'I suppose it comforts me a lot because he's been with me through everything, so it's a very stable presence. It reminds me of being at home with friends and family' (p. 29). Objects may also be physically hard but highly portable and wearable, for example two silver bracelets (one charm bracelet and one bangle), which elicited the comment, 'I get some of the same comfort from wearing these two bracelets as I would from speaking to my parents or grandad' (p. 29).

The creation of something as a gift can be particularly important, as in the case of a 3D-printed elephant 'My brother made it for me when I left home for undergraduate, I've kept it the whole time ... It just reminds me of home when I feel homesick' (Bell and Spikins, 2018: 29).

Historically, archaeologists such as Bell and Spikins (2018) in their research have explored how objects affect us emotionally. Psychological research has revealed that objects can have powerful effects on emotional well-being, acting as attachment figures which provide a sense of comfort and security in the absence of loved ones, and promoting the confidence to explore and develop positive relationships. In Bell and Spikins' (2008: 30) study, the understanding about attachment objects was applied as a new interpretation of two particularly meaningful prehistoric artefacts. These were known as the Stonehenge pig 'toy'. The Stonehenge pig attracted attention as 'Britain's oldest toy' (Owen, 2008). However, neither the concept of a toy, plaything or an art object allows for the potential emotional significance TO may hold for both infants and their caregivers. This small object may have been far more significant than simply something with which to engage in and pretend play. Bell and Spikins (2008) concluded that while they cannot confirm these were cherished or sentimental toys, they were often found in graves, next to the bones of young children. They concluded that a better understanding of attachment objects will provide considerable insight into the emotional significance of cherished artefacts.

In thinking through a Rhizoanalysis lens, it could have been something carved with sentimental value and then given to the child in the form of the mid-20th-century term, Transitional Object, providing the infant with feelings of comfort and security, in times of separation. Although this cannot conclusively be determined either way it highlights possibilities perhaps less considered in disciplines beyond psychology and child development (Bell and Spikins, 2018).

A Final Note

This chapter has aimed to offer an alternative lens to TO and the way they are perceived through the lens of the adult, the child, and also other disciplines. It has included several research projects to highlight the continuing interest around TO in modern day society. The value of TO in different contexts was also considered and perhaps this is an area for further consideration, including children going on holidays or those seeking temporary objects for coping with, for example bereavement and loss, discussed in this and the previous chapter.

This chapter offers definitions of objects, including Transitional Objects, as:

• Objects of attachment.
• Temporal objects.
• Transient objects.
• The biographies of objects.

By exploring the themes discussed in this chapter, the topic for future consideration could therefore be exploring the cultural attachment to objects in the 21st century.

References

Bell, T. and Spikins, P. (2018) The object of my affection: attachments security and material culture. *Time and Mind*, 11 (1): 23–39. https://doi.org/10.1080/1751696X.2018.1433355

Bowlby, J. (1969) *Attachment and Loss, Vol. 1: Attachment*. New York: Basic Books.

Bowlby, J. (1988) *A Secure Base: Clinical Applications of Attachment Theory*. London: Routledge.

Deleuze, G. and Guattari, F. (2014) Rhizome. In J. J. Gieseking, W. Mangold, C. Katz, S. Low, and S. Saegert (eds), *The People, Place, and Space Reader*. London: Routledge, 403–406.

Gillath, O., Karantzas, G. C., and Fraley, R. C. (2016) *Adult Attachment: A Concise Introduction to Theory and Research*. Cambridge, MA: Academic Press.

Isaacs, D. and Isaacs, S. (2014) Transitional objects. *Paediatric Child Health*, 50: 845–846. https://doi.org/10.1111/jpc.12747

LeDuff, III, L. D., Bradshaw, W. T., and Blake, S. M. (2017) Transitional objects to facilitate grieving following perinatal loss. *Advances in Neonatal Care*, 17 (5): 347–353. https://doi.org/10.1097/ANC.0000000000000429

Lehman, E. B., Denham, S. A., Moser, M. H., and Reeves, S. L. (1992) Soft object and pacifier attachments in young children: The role of security of attachment to the mother. *Journal of Child Psychology and Psychiatry*, 33: 1205–1215. https://doi.org/10.1111/j.1469-7610.1992.tb00939

Lehman, E. B., Arnold, B. E., Reeves, S. L., and Steier, A. (1996) Maternal beliefs about children's attachments to soft objects. *American Journal of Orthopsychiatry*, 66 (3): 427–436.

Leitner, K. (2016) Children's use of transitional objects in paediatric healthcare settings: Policies and practices. Master's thesis, November 2016, East Carolina University. Available at: https://thescholarship.ecu.edu/bitstream/handle/10342/6035/LEITNER-MASTERSTHESIS-2016.pdf?sequence=1

Litt, C. J. (1986) Theories of transitional object attachment: an overview. *International Journal of Behavioral Development*, 9: 383–399. https://doi.org/10.1177/016502548600900308

Olsson, L. M. (2009) *Movement and Experimentation in Young Children's Learning: Deleuze and Guattari in Early Childhood Education*. New York: Routledge.

Owen, J. (2008) Britain's oldest toy found buried with Stonehenge baby? *National Geographic*, October 21. Available at: https://news.nationalgeographic.com/news/2008/10/081021-stonehenge-toy.html (accessed November 24, 2017).

Perry, M. (2021) Transitional objects: Teddy bears relieve stress in children. *The Bear Blog*, October 28. Available at: www.bearsforhumanity.com/blogs/bear-blog/transitional-objects-teddy-bears-as-a-way-to-relieve-stress-in-children

Sarner, M. (2018) Still have your childhood teddy? The psychological power of the toys we keep. *The Guardian*, December 12. Available at: www.theguardian.com/society/2018/dec/12/still-have-childhood-teddy-psychological-power-toys-we-keep (accessed September 28, 2023).

Scherer, L. and Norman, A. (2023) The sleeping voices: Evaluating parenting 'self-help' books, narratives of rule, routine and ritual. *Children & Society*, 37 (4): 1203–1217. https://doi.org/10.1111/chso.12714

Sellars, M. (2013) *Young Children Becoming Curriculum: Deleuze, Te Whariki and Curricular Understandings*. New York: Routledge.

Triebenbacher, S. L. and Tegano, D. W. (1993) Children's use of transitional objects during daily separations from significant caregivers. *Perceptual and Motor Skills*, 76: 89–90. https://doi.org/10.2466/pms.1993.76.1.89

Winnicott, D. W. (1953) Transitional objects and transitional phenomena: A study of the first not-me possession. *The International Journal of Psychoanalysis*, 34: 89–97.

Winnicott, D. W. (1960) The theory of the parent–infant relationship. In *The Maturational Processes and the Facilitating Environment*. New York: International University Press.

Chapter 8

Concluding Note

Looking Back, Moving Forward

Care and tuned-in relationships (Trevarthen, 1993) are key to early childhood education and yet the therapeutic approaches to support emotions are often predominately left to external experts or for those undertaking specific training in addition to their early year's qualifications achieved. All the chapters in this book have aimed to guide the reader through the potentials of understanding the significance of objects that children desire to have close to them in regulating their own emotions and well-being. The book has therefore examined young children's emotional states in connection to TOs. It has revealed how a therapeutic approach and relationship within psychoanalysis could be understood and weaved within early years professional practice and how this could enrich experiences for children and educators. The book therefore has aimed to include an exploration about how early years professionals can support the children in their care by holding them in mind, valuing their ideas and selves, and creating a nurturing environment. By focusing on relationships, attachment and object relations connections have been made to understand and inform practices related to child development and TO.

Application to Practice and What We Can Learn about TOs: An Approach in Working with Children

The model in Figure 8.1 aims to provide a working infographic from each of the chapter's contents and to illustrate the areas considered.

What Is My Position as Author and Researcher in This Book?

As a psychologist and educator embedded in research and practice I was always interested in the differing perspectives of understanding children's behaviour and the connections to development, emotions, and understanding. I firmly position myself as a Froebelian educator – the child at the heart of their educational experience, the connection to nature, and the value of play are essential to growth and development. This aligns with my thinking about person centredness and how attachment informs my pedagogical thinking. In turning to attachment and the importance relationships play, I have moved beyond humans to

DOI: 10.4324/9781003296669-11

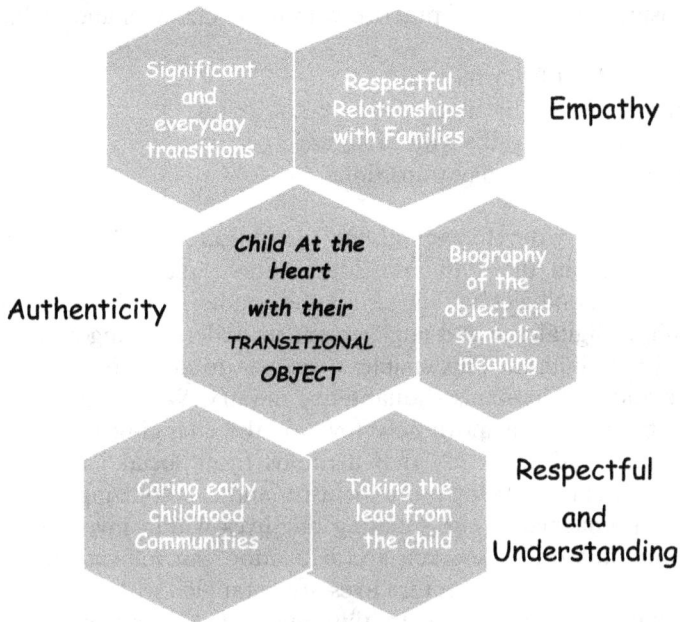

Figure 8.1 A caring approach with children and transitional objects. Policies in early years settings to develop a relational approach and acceptance of Transitional Objects.

considering the non-human objects individuals place value on. This widens my thinking towards what I mean by 'objects' and has taken me on a journey in exploring and reflecting on Winnicott's understandings about TOs. I had some previous knowledge about this but, similarly to other professionals, it remained superficial and was embedded in the psychological psychodynamic perspective of one of many theories I had read. By being given the opportunity by The Squiggle Trust to have some time to read and talk to professionals in early years education further, I have made more connections and travelled down many more paths than I had anticipated. I have therefore aimed to try to remain true to Winnicott's TO and their meanings in early childhood. However, I have also branched out a little and wanted to include the distinction between sentimental objects, the everlasting relationships other than human relationships, and what disciplines beyond psychology have to say about non-human objects and children living in the 21st century. I therefore offer a model of practice – as an infographic about the principles of care, being:

- Authentic.
- Empatheticy.
- Respectful and understanding.

Whilst considering aspects of practice within the chapters and including:

- Taking the lead from the child.
- Biography of the object and symbolic meaning.
- Respectful relationships with families.
- Significant and everyday transitions.

Similarly to the way developmental and sociological perspectives formed new forms of inquiry in the 19th and 20th century, the 21st century includes innovative methodologies within childhood studies. In the 21st century we move within a digital age and engagement to understanding and researching with and about children. This enables discourse to develop that reimagines a humanist's and non-humanists' qualitative inquiry. Where once research was deemed stable there is a move now towards the changing forces of research that challenges traditional research methods from social justice and equity perspectives – the focus being more inclusive and decolonizing as regards how research is approached. By re-situating our lives within invisible, more than human common worlds, research and education can refocus on the ways in which our past, present, and future lives are entangled with other beings, non-living entities, and technology. In thinking from a feminist perspective, it draws differently on scholarship as well as thinking with indigenous knowledge of histories and territories. By making the visible public, in this book how we value, understand, and approach the connection between the child and their TO, the personal and private is always political and the mundane everyday acts matter. It reminds us that power is not equitably distributed as we live and how we become through a series of relations. This is why I have included the central model with the reminder that in all we do the child is at the heart, with their TO. What also emerges in common worlds method and more broadly as we work in early years with children, is that researchers are understood as embedded within the entangled life worlds they seek to explore, researching to learn with rather than learn about. The research I hope is not ideas and methods brought in and applied to research but understood and reflected on through the lived process itself.

Reference

Trevarthen, C. (1993) The self born in intersubjectivity: The psychology of an infant communicating. In U. Neisser (ed.), *The Perceived Self: Ecological and Interpersonal Sources of Self-knowledge.* Cambridge: Cambridge University Press, 121–173.

Index

Note: Page numbers in *italics* refer to figures.

For Product Safety Concerns and Information please contact our EU
representative GPSR@taylorandfrancis.com
Taylor & Francis Verlag GmbH, Kaufingerstraße 24, 80331 München, Germany

www.ingramcontent.com/pod-product-compliance
Lightning Source LLC
Chambersburg PA
CBHW050612280326
41932CB00016B/3019